DOING GROUNDED THEORY

D1600340

Doing Grounded Theory by Uwe Flick is the eighth volume in *The SAGE Qualitative Research Kit*. This book can be used together with the other titles in the *Kit* as a comprehensive guide to the process of doing qualitative research, but is equally valuable on its own as a practical introduction to doing grounded theory.

Fully updated and expanded to ten volumes, this second edition of the *Kit* presents the most extensive introduction to the state-of-the-art of qualitative research.

COMPLETE LIST OF TITLES IN *THE SAGE QUALITATIVE RESEARCH KIT*

- *Designing Qualitative Research* **Uwe Flick**
- *Doing Interviews* **Svend Brinkmann and Steinar Kvale**
- *Doing Ethnography* **Amanda Coffey**
- *Doing Focus Groups* **Rosaline Barbour**
- *Using Visual Data in Qualitative Research* **Marcus Banks**
- *Analyzing Qualitative Data* **Graham R. Gibbs**
- *Doing Conversation, Discourse and Document Analysis* **Tim Rapley**
- *Doing Grounded Theory* **Uwe Flick**
- *Doing Triangulation and Mixed Methods* **Uwe Flick**
- *Managing Quality in Qualitative Research* **Uwe Flick**

MEMBERS OF THE EDITORIAL ADVISORY BOARD

Kathy Charmaz	Sonoma University, USA
Amanda Coffey	Cardiff University, UK
John Creswell	University of Nebraska-Lincoln, USA
Norman K. Denzin	University of Illinois, Urbana Champaign, USA
Sonia Livingstone	London School of Economics, UK
Joseph A. Maxwell	George Mason University, USA
Michael Murray	Keele University, UK
Judith Preissle	University of Georgia, USA
Clive Seale	Brunel University, UK

DOING GROUNDED THEORY

UWE FLICK

THE SAGE QUALITATIVE RESEARCH KIT 2ND EDITION

Edited by Uwe Flick

Los Angeles | London | New Delhi
Singapore | Washington DC | Melbourne

BRESCIA UNIVERSITY
COLLEGE LIBRARY

Los Angeles | London | New Delhi
Singapore | Washington DC | Melbourne

SAGE Publications Ltd
1 Oliver's Yard
55 City Road
London EC1Y 1SP

SAGE Publications Inc.
2455 Teller Road
Thousand Oaks, California 91320

SAGE Publications India Pvt Ltd
B 1/I 1 Mohan Cooperative Industrial Area
Mathura Road
New Delhi 110 044

SAGE Publications Asia-Pacific Pte Ltd
3 Church Street
#10-04 Samsung Hub
Singapore 049483

© Uwe Flick 2018

Apart from any fair dealing for the purposes of research
or private study, or criticism or review, as permitted
under the Copyright, Designs and Patents Act, 1988, this
publication may be reproduced, stored or transmitted in
any form, or by any means, only with the prior permission
in writing of the publishers, or in the case of reprographic
reproduction, in accordance with the terms of licences
issued by the Copyright Licensing Agency. Enquiries
concerning reproduction outside those terms should be
sent to the publishers.

Editor: Mila Steele
Editorial assistant: John Nightingale
Production editor: Victoria Nicholas
Copyeditor: Andy Baxter
Proofreader: Thea Watson
Marketing manager: Emma Turner
Cover design: Shaun Mercier
Typeset by C&M Digitals (P) Ltd, Chennai, India
Printed in the UK

Library of Congress Control Number: 2017941093

British Library Cataloguing in Publication data

A catalogue record for this book is available from
the British Library

ISBN 978-1-4739-1200-7 (pbk)

At SAGE we take sustainability seriously. Most of our products are printed in the UK using FSC papers and boards.
When we print overseas we ensure sustainable papers are used as measured by the PREPS grading system.
We undertake an annual audit to monitor our sustainability.

UNIVERSITY
COLLEGE LIBRARY

CONTENTS

LIST OF ILLUSTRATIONS

BOXES

FIGURES

TABLE

EDITORIAL INTRODUCTION

UWE FLICK

INTRODUCTION TO *THE SAGE QUALITATIVE RESEARCH KIT*

In recent years, qualitative research has enjoyed a period of unprecedented growth and diversification as it has become an established and respected research approach across a variety of disciplines and contexts. An increasing number of students, teachers and practitioners are facing questions and problems of how to do qualitative research – in general and for their specific individual purposes. To answer these questions, and to address such practical problems on a how-to-do level, is the main purpose of *The SAGE Qualitative Research Kit*.

The books in *The SAGE Qualitative Research Kit* collectively address the core issues that arise when we actually do qualitative research. Each book focuses on key methods (e.g. interviews or focus groups) or materials (e.g. visual data or discourse) that are used for studying the social world in qualitative terms. Moreover, the books in the *Kit* have been written with the needs of many different types of reader in mind. As such, the *Kit* and the individual books will be of use to a wide variety of users:

- *Practitioners* of qualitative research in the social sciences; medical research; marketing research; evaluation; organizational, business and management studies; cognitive science; etc., who face the problem of planning and conducting a specific study using qualitative methods.
- *University teachers* and lecturers in these fields using qualitative methods can use this series as a basis of their teaching.
- *Undergraduate and graduate students* of social sciences, nursing, education, psychology and other fields where qualitative methods are a (main) part of the university training including practical applications (e.g. when writing a thesis).

Each book in *The SAGE Qualitative Research Kit* has been written by distinguished authors with extensive experience in their field and in practice with the methods they write about. When reading the whole series of books from the beginning to the end, you will repeatedly come across some issues which are central to any sort of qualitative research – such as ethics, designing research or assessing quality. However, in each book such issues are addressed from the specific methodological angle of the authors and the approach they describe. Thus you may find different approaches to issues of quality or different suggestions for how to analyze qualitative data in different books, which will combine to present a comprehensive picture of the field as a whole.

WHAT IS QUALITATIVE RESEARCH?

It has become more and more difficult to find a common definition of qualitative research which is accepted by the majority of qualitative research approaches and researchers. Qualitative research is no longer just simply '*not* quantitative research', but has developed an identity (or maybe multiple identities) of its own.

Despite the multiplicity of approaches to qualitative research, some common features of qualitative research can be identified. Qualitative research is intended to approach the world 'out there' (not in specialized research settings such as laboratories) and to understand, describe and sometimes explain social phenomena 'from the inside' in a number of different ways:

- By analyzing experiences of individuals or groups. Experiences can be related to biographical life histories or to (everyday or professional) practices; they may be addressed by analyzing everyday knowledge, accounts and stories.
- By analyzing interactions and communications in the making. This can be based on observing or recording practices of interacting and communicating and analyzing this material.
- By analyzing documents (texts, images, film or music) or similar traces of experiences or interactions.

Common to such approaches is that they seek to unpick how people construct the world around them, what they are doing or what is happening to them in terms that are meaningful and that offer rich insight. Interactions and documents are seen as ways of constituting social processes and artefacts collaboratively (or conflictingly). All of these approaches represent ways of meaning, which can be reconstructed and analyzed with different qualitative methods that allow the researcher to develop (more or less generalizable) models, typologies, theories as ways of describing and explaining social (or psychological) issues.

HOW DO WE CONDUCT QUALITATIVE RESEARCH?

Can we identify common ways of doing qualitative research if we take into account that there are different theoretical, epistemological and methodological approaches to qualitative research and that the issues that are studied are very diverse as well? We can at least identify some common features of how qualitative research is done.

- Qualitative researchers are interested in accessing experiences, interactions and documents in their natural context and in a way that gives room to the particularities of them and the materials in which they are studied.
- Qualitative research refrains from setting up a well-defined concept of what is studied and from formulating hypotheses in the beginning in order to test them. Rather, concepts (or hypotheses, if they are used) are developed and refined in the process of research.
- Qualitative research starts from the idea that methods and theories should be appropriate to what is studied. If the existing methods do not fit with a concrete issue or field, they are adapted or new methods or approaches are developed.
- Researchers themselves are an important part of the research process, either in terms of their own personal presence as researchers, or in terms of their experiences in the field and with the reflexivity they bring to the role – as are members of the field under study.
- Qualitative research takes context and cases seriously for understanding an issue under study. A lot of qualitative research is based on case studies or a series of case studies, and often the case (its history and complexity) is an important context for understanding what is studied.
- A major part of qualitative research is based on texts and writing – from field notes and transcripts to descriptions and interpretations and finally to the presentation of the findings and of the research as a whole. Therefore, issues of transforming complex social situations (or other materials such as images) into texts – issues of transcribing and writing in general – are major concerns of qualitative research.
- If methods are supposed to be adequate to what is under study, approaches to defining and assessing the quality of qualitative research (still) have to be discussed in specific ways that are appropriate for qualitative research and even for specific approaches in qualitative research.

SCOPE OF *THE SAGE QUALITATIVE RESEARCH KIT*

Designing Qualitative Research (Uwe Flick) gives a brief introduction to qualitative research from the point of view of how to plan and design a concrete study using qualitative research in one way or another. It is intended to outline a framework for the other books in *The SAGE Qualitative Research Kit* by focusing on how-to-do problems and on how to solve such problems in the research process. The book addresses issues of constructing a research design in qualitative research; it outlines stumbling blocks in making a research project work and discusses practical problems such as resources in qualitative research but also more methodological issues like the quality of qualitative research and also ethics. This framework is filled out in more detail in the other books in the *Kit*.

Three books are devoted to collecting or producing data in qualitative research. They take up the issues briefly outlined in the first book and approach them in a much more detailed and focused way for the specific method. First, *Doing Interviews* (Svend Brinkmann and Steinar Kvale) addresses the theoretical, epistemological, ethical and practical issues of interviewing people about specific issues or their life history. *Doing Ethnography* (Amanda Coffey) focuses on the second major approach to collecting and producing qualitative data. Here again practical issues (like selecting sites, methods of collecting data in ethnography, special problems of analyzing them) are discussed in the context of more general issues (ethics, representations, quality and adequacy of ethnography as an approach). In *Doing Focus Groups* (Rosaline Barbour) the third of the most important qualitative methods of producing data is presented. Here again we find a strong focus on how-to-do issues of sampling, designing and analyzing the data and on how to produce them in focus groups.

Three further volumes are devoted to analyzing specific types of qualitative data. *Using Visual Data in Qualitative Research* (Marcus Banks) extends the focus to the third type of qualitative data (beyond verbal data coming from interviews and focus groups and observational data). The use of visual data has not only become a major trend in social research in general, but confronts researchers with new practical problems in using them and analyzing them and produces new ethical issues. In *Analyzing Qualitative Data* (Graham R. Gibbs), several practical approaches and issues of making sense of any sort of qualitative data are addressed. Special attention is paid to practices of coding, of comparing and of using computer-assisted qualitative data analysis. Here, the focus is on verbal data, like interviews, focus groups or biographies. *Doing Conversation, Discourse and Document Analysis* (Tim Rapley) extends this focus to different types of data, relevant for analyzing discourses. Here, the focus is on existing material (like documents) and on recording everyday conversations and on finding traces of discourses. Practical issues such as generating an archive, transcribing video materials and how to analyze discourses with such types of data are discussed.

Three final volumes go beyond specific forms of data or single methods and take a broader approach. *Doing Grounded Theory* (Uwe Flick) focuses on an integrated research programme in qualitative research. *Doing Triangulation and Mixed Methods* (Uwe Flick) addresses combinations of several approaches in qualitative research or with quantitative methods. *Managing Quality in Qualitative Research* (Uwe Flick) takes up the issue of quality in qualitative research, which has been briefly addressed in specific contexts in other books in the *Kit*, in a more general way. Here, quality is looked at from the angle of using or reformulating existing criteria, or defining new criteria for qualitative research. This book examines the ongoing debates about what should count as defining 'quality' and validity in qualitative methodologies and examines the many strategies for promoting and managing quality in qualitative research.

Before I go on to outline the focus of this book and its role in the *Kit*, I would like to thank some people at SAGE who were important in making this *Kit* happen. Michael Carmichael suggested this project to me some time ago and was very helpful with his suggestions in the beginning. Patrick Brindle, Katie Metzler and Mila Steele took over and continued this support, as did Victoria Nicholas and John Nightingale in making books out of the manuscripts we provided.

ABOUT THIS BOOK

UWE FLICK

Grounded theory was developed as a research programme more than 50 years ago. It has been a major part of the growing and always proliferating field of qualitative research and qualitative methods. It is often associated with being a specific approach mainly to analyzing qualitative data. However, *doing grounded theory* covers more than that. It can be seen as a comprehensive research programme with a specific understanding of the research process, of selecting materials and using and producing qualitative data. Grounded theory is distinct from other qualitative research programmes because of its major aim – to develop theories from empirical analyses and to provide explanations for phenomena. Since its early days, this programme has been proliferating within itself. Since at least the 1990s we have had more than one understanding of what grounded theory is about, how coding, for example, should be done and the like. These versions of grounded theory stand side by side and in competition with each other. At the same time, grounded theory and its versions can be inspiring for other approaches in qualitative research as well – for example, for how to do qualitative data analysis (Gibbs, 2018). It can be stimulating for doing ethnography (Coffey, 2018) and it can be linked to research combining several qualitative or quantitative methods (Flick, 2018a). It has its own ideas about the quality of qualitative research (see Flick, 2018b), which are relevant for other areas of qualitative research, too. Whereas the other books in *The SAGE Qualitative Research Kit* focus on one particular method of data collection (such as focus groups – Barbour, 2018 – or interviews – Brinkmann and Kvale, 2018) or on one step in the process (such as collecting data in interviews and focus groups or analyzing qualitative data – Gibbs, 2018), this book is about a more integrated approach. However, the link to the other books in *The SAGE Qualitative Research Kit* is that all these methods can become relevant for doing grounded theory. In this sense, the book has two functions in the context of the *Kit*: as a stand-alone book it aims to give a short, but comprehensive introduction to *doing grounded theory* and the several versions available; as an addition to the other books in the *Kit*, it rounds out the framework of the other books at a methodological level from a more integrative perspective on doing qualitative research.

CHAPTER ONE

BACKGROUND

APPROACHES AND PHILOSOPHIES OF GROUNDED THEORY

CONTENTS

CHAPTER OBJECTIVES

After reading this chapter, you should understand:

- the history and background of grounded theory;
- the versions that have developed over the years;
- some essentials of the philosophies behind these versions;
- the differences between discovering and constructing grounded theory;
- the problematic issue of using existing literature;
- what theory means in this context; and
- when to use grounded theory research.

INTRODUCTION

The idea behind this book is to take you on a journey through grounded theory research to give you some orientation on how to begin, plan and do your own, maybe first, study in the context of grounded theory. For this purpose we will look at the phases of a grounded theory study from two angles. In Chapters 3–7, we will look for the methodological and practical advice the methodological literature about grounded theory gives you for doing your project (e.g. concerning data collection). And if concrete advice is limited, we will turn to the second angle and add such concrete advice from the more general literature in qualitative research. In the last part of the book (Chapters 8 and 9) you will find some suggestions for how to conceive your study more systematically. Before we go into the more practical aspects of doing grounded theory, the first two chapters will give you a short overview about the process and elements of doing grounded theory (see Chapter 2). First, this chapter addresses the background of grounded theory and outlines how the field has developed, to give you a basic orientation about what grounded theory is, and what you can refer to for your own project.

WHAT IS GROUNDED THEORY?

Grounded theory as a term has featured in the discussion about qualitative research for five decades. Barney Glaser and Anselm Strauss established it as a label with a monograph (Glaser and Strauss, 1967), which describes the research style the authors had used in a number of studies (e.g. 1965a) with or without using this label (e.g. Strauss et al., 1964). The term is used for three purposes: to label a certain type of theory, which has been developed from analyzing empirical material (a grounded theory of …); or a specific methodological approach (grounded theory methodology according to …); or a specific process and attitude in the field (doing grounded theory according to …). More recently, this approach was summarized as having four features: minimal preconceptions about the issue under study, simultaneous data collection and analysis, using various interpretations for data, and aiming at constructing middle range theories as the outcome of the research (e.g. Charmaz, 2008).

HISTORY AND BACKGROUND OF GROUNDED THEORY RESEARCH

Grounded theory was developed by two researchers with differing backgrounds but common interests in distinction from the existing landscape of research. The background of Anselm Strauss was in the **Chicago School of Sociology**, whereas Glaser came from Columbia University. The distinctions they were interested in were in two directions. First, against the mainstream of sociological research, which was starting from (grand or middle range) theories aiming at empirically testing existing theories but not interested in how theories were developed or engaged in developing new theories. The original orientation of grounded theory was outlined by Glaser and Strauss in distinction to this understanding and based on the conviction that the main task for sociology at that time was to discover theories. A second point of reference was the practice in **ethnography** at that time, which mainly provided detailed descriptions of situations, fields, institutions, etc., but no explanations or theoretical models for analyzing why something happened and what consequences it had. Glaser and Strauss outlined their alternative programme according to Bryant and Charmaz (2007a, p. 31) in four 'founding texts': *Awareness of Dying* (Glaser and Strauss 1965a), *The Discovery of Grounded Theory* (Glaser and Strauss, 1967), *Time for Dying* (Glaser and Strauss, 1968) and *Status Passage* (Glaser and Strauss, 1971). The 1967 book is less a textbook (as it is seen today) than a programmatic statement, although it includes many essentials of the method as it was developed later and currently is used or should be used. The other books by Glaser and Strauss (1965a, 1968, 1971) are studies applying this programme but are mainly oriented on a practical problem that is studied (the organization of interaction with and about dying patients in hospitals, see Case study 1.1).

CASE STUDY 1.1 AWARENESS OF DYING – APPROACH

The following example represents one of the first and major studies using this form of research process with the goal of developing theories from qualitative research in the field. Barney Glaser and Anselm Strauss did this study in the context of medical sociology in several hospitals in the USA around San Francisco. Their research question was what influenced various persons' interaction with dying people and how the knowledge – that the person would die soon – determined the interaction with that person. More concretely, they studied the forms of interaction between the dying person and the clinical staff in the hospital, between the staff and the relatives, and between relatives and the dying person.

The starting point of the research was the observation, when the researchers' own relatives were in hospital, that the staff in hospitals (at that time) seemed not to inform the patients with a terminal disease and their relatives about the status and the life expectancy of the patient. Rather, the possibility that the patient might die or die soon was treated as taboo. This general observation and the questions it raised were taken as a starting point for more systematic observation and interviews in one hospital. These data were analyzed and used to develop categories. That was also the background for deciding to include another hospital and to continue the data collection and analysis there. Both hospitals, as cases, were immediately compared for similarities and differences.

Results of such comparison were used to decide which hospital to research next, until finally six hospitals were included in the study. These included a teaching hospital, a Veterans Administration hospital, two county hospitals, a private Catholic hospital and a state hospital. Wards included, among others, geriatrics, cancer, intensive care, paediatrics and neurosurgery and the fieldworkers stayed two to four weeks in each. The data from each of these units (different wards in one hospital, similar wards in different hospitals, hospitals among each other) were contrasted and compared to show similarities and differences.

At the end of the study, comparable situations and contexts outside hospitals and health care were included as another dimension of comparison. Analyzing and comparing the data allowed the development of a theoretical model, which then was transferred to other fields in order to develop it further. The result of this study was a theory of awareness contexts as ways of dealing with the information and with the patients' needs to know more about their situation. Details of the results will be outlined later in Case study 2.1, and ways of analyzing the data will be discussed further in Chapter 4.

This study provides a good example of using the research process outlined in this book to develop theoretically relevant insights from a series of case studies and their comparison (see Glaser and Strauss, 1965a, for details). Here, theory was not a starting point: there was no theory available at that time to explain the initial experiences of the researchers with their own relatives in hospital. Theory was the end product of the research, and it was developed out of empirical material and the analysis of this material.

Glaser and Strauss were not the only ones at that time who were unhappy with the mainstream of research in the social sciences and in particular in sociology. They formulated their programme in a period when other important programmes for qualitative research were developed, such as Harold Garfinkel's *Studies in* **Ethnomethodology** (1967), Goffman's studies (1961, 1963) and more general books like Berger and Luckmann's (1966) *The Social Construction of Reality* or Thomas Kuhn's *The Structure of Scientific Revolutions* (1962). It would be beyond the limits of this introduction to go into details of these publications, but they defined a climate of theoretical and methodological change. Glaser and Strauss formulated their programme in San Francisco in a world which was in upheaval in other contexts as well (the counterculture of 1967). All this means that they were not alone with their alternative programme of doing social research but relatively quickly became part of the broader programme of rediscovering qualitative research, although Glaser always mentioned that their programme also referred to quantitative research and data. But being part of a broader qualitative research movement motivated the distinctions between qualitative research and grounded theory (e.g. in Glaser, 2001). After Glaser and Strauss's joint invention of this term, four developments characterize the following decades. First, a further elaboration of the methodology can be noted. This elaboration comes from the founding fathers' more and more separate efforts but also from the second generation (researchers such as Kathy Charmaz, Juliet Corbin, Judith Holton, Adele Clarke and Janice Morse) of grounded theory (see Morse et al., 2009). Second, the growing success of grounded theory has led to a diversification of the field. We find researchers who apply the method as it was conceived or further developed by one of these protagonists. But we can also see an interesting progression of the concept 'grounded theory' as a metaphor for doing qualitative research, for **coding** material and the like. Third, we find a, sometimes harsh, debate about what grounded theory is and what is the right way to do it. This again has led to a proliferation of several versions of grounded theory and continuous critiques in one direction or another. Fourth, there are efforts to reconcile the debates and fights, to unite the field again (e.g. in *The SAGE Handbook of Grounded Theory* – Bryant and Charmaz, 2007b) and to anchor the approach more firmly in the broader field of qualitative research. In particular, Charmaz has not tired of contributing chapters to all the most important handbooks, and papers to the most important conferences in the field.

CURRENT VERSIONS OF GROUNDED THEORY RESEARCH

The consequence of the developments outlined above is that now at least five versions of grounded theory as a **research programme** exist:

- The original version designed by Glaser and Strauss together in *The Discovery of Grounded Theory* (1967) oriented on creating a new understanding of research and focused on empirically developing a theory with a core category.
- The further development of many of these ideas by Glaser (1978) in his book *Theoretical Sensitivity*. In the long run, this led to what is now called 'classic grounded theory' and presented in Glaser's later books (e.g. 1992, 1998) and most recently by Holton and Walsh (2017).
- Some years after Glaser, Strauss (1987) started to develop his own approach of *Qualitative Analysis for Social Scientists*, in which he adapted several of Glaser's additions to the methodology and skipped others. This string of grounded theory was further developed in publications with Juliet Corbin (Strauss and Corbin, 1990) and is now advanced by Corbin (Corbin and Strauss, 2015). In recent editions of their textbook, several of Strauss's ideas and many of those Glaser had initiated have been abandoned. This version attracted most attention in the 1990s, but provoked harsh critiques by Glaser from the 1990s onward.
- The fourth version has been developed by Kathy Charmaz using the label constructivist grounded theory in her book *Constructing Grounded Theory* (2014, originally 2006) and in *The SAGE Handbook of Grounded Theory* (Bryant and Charmaz, 2007b). These publications also aim at reintegrating both Strauss (and Corbin) and Glaser into a comprehensive version of grounded theory.
- The fifth version comes from Adele Clarke (2005) in her book *Situational Analysis*. Clarke has turned grounded theory into a postmodernist version focusing more on situations, social arenas and discourses than on theory development in the sense of Glaser and Strauss.

These five versions exist side by side and in competition, and complement each other with their methodological suggestions (for how to code for example). This makes it appealing to have a look at the various versions and what they suggest for how to proceed in conceiving your own studies, and collecting and analyzing data (see Chapters 2–6). However, they also represent differing philosophies of and behind grounded theory research.

THE PHILOSOPHIES OF GROUNDED THEORY RESEARCH

Classic grounded theory – the claim for pure discovery

The approach of classic grounded theory in the tradition of Glaser's work over the years does not pay (much) attention to **epistemology** or theories of knowledge, as the following statement from an interview with Glaser highlights: 'Epistemology. A theory of – or a theoretical perspective. That's all bullshit for grounded theory. You can read it in *Theoretical Coding*. GT is just a stupid little method. That's all it is. The epistemology is irrelevant. It's how you use it' (Glaser, 2007a, p. 27). The epistemological programme of Glaser's approach is rather empiricist: data are seen as data. Methods for collecting data do not play a systematic role. The principle for developing codes, new theories or new knowledge is **induction** – all is in the data. All categories should be derived from observation of phenomena. You should go as open minded as possible into the field, where you collect what you find as data. 'All is data' is another dictum by Glaser (1992). The main principles to understand are emergence and discovery. Both assume that data and relevant facts are already 'there' and you simply collect them. Any thoughts about the role of methods as part of the process of identifying something as data or as relevant are ignored or seen as obstacles to the right way of discovering. As Kelle has repeatedly criticized (e.g. 2014), this is a kind of naïve empiricism, which is characterized in a specific form of belief in the data and in the pure inductive process of discovery, in which all that is relevant simply emerges. Although Glaser is sceptical about methodological instruments such as the ones suggested by Strauss later (see Chapter 4), he has also developed tools you can use for his kind of analysis (e.g. the **coding families** he suggested – see also Chapter 4).

Canonization of grounded theory research – inductive and deductive approaches

Strauss (1987), and later Strauss and Corbin (1990), have invested further thought into developing methodological instruments – such as the **coding paradigm** (see Chapter 4) – to develop a structure from the observations in the material and in particular between categories. In their approach, they also emphasize an inductive understanding of the relation between phenomena and categorization in particular in their first form of coding (open coding, see Chapter 4), but they also are aware that the process includes more and more elements of **deduction**. Phenomena are coded in already developed categories. Specific forms of relations between categories can be helpful for the analysis and so on. Strauss has also put a strong emphasis on the interpretation of phenomena – by both the research participants and the researchers. In 1995, Strauss and Corbin had written a text clarifying the methodological assumptions behind grounded theory (in Strauss's view). This text was originally written for the second edition of their book (1998) as a theoretical introduction. After Strauss's death in 1996 it was not included in the book. This text consists of 16 methodological assumptions. After excerpts showed up in later editions of Corbin and Strauss's book in varying degrees of completeness, the whole text (Strauss and Corbin, 2016) was published in English as a chapter in a German book. These assumptions can be reduced to four major points. (1) Symbolic meanings are represented and produced in interactions through actions and have to be renegotiated if differences emerge. (2) Human activities occur along routines. However, if contingencies occur, this is repaired by active reflection so that habitual actions can continue. (3) Internal, external, past, current and future conditions impact on actions (such as the actor's biography, emotions, current or anticipated occurrences). (4) Actions are embedded in chains of interactions with phases or stages, and conditions, perspectives and meanings can change (see also Griesbacher, 2016, pp. 145–6). These assumptions provide the background and explanations for the tools Strauss and Corbin developed for analyzing material – e.g. the coding paradigm (see Chapter 4). They show a background in **symbolic interactionism** and stress the role of interpretations by people involved in actions and interactions and the researcher's interpretation in the analysis. At the same time, these assumptions provide reasons why Strauss always emphasized and defended the role of deduction (i.e. the allocation of material to existing categories) in the analytic process – for example, by using the coding paradigm. For him (and Corbin), induction (the consequent development of categories from the material to be analyzed) was not enough for analyzing phenomena and for developing theories from it. As Bryant and Charmaz (2007a, p. 46) note (and discuss in more detail), Strauss was influenced by Dewey, Peirce, Mead and Blumer. Research for him is moving from induction when developing concepts from data, to deduction by clarifying the concepts with extended collection of data which are allocated to the already developed concepts. This shows how grounded theory, which was originally strongly committed to a consistently inductive approach (and still is in Glaser's version – see above), has turned into an inductive–deductive approach in the version of Strauss and Corbin.

Mild constructivism and pragmatism as backgrounds

Charmaz's approach of a constructivist grounded theory builds both on Glaser and on Strauss and tries to advance both their versions in overcoming some epistemological shortcomings. In their later writings, Strauss and Corbin already noted that 'theories are always traceable to the data that gave rise to them – within the interactive context of data collection and data analyzing, in which the analyst is also a crucially significant interactant' (1994, pp. 278–9). Although Strauss always had a background in **pragmatism**, Charmaz, together with Bryant or with Thornberg, emphasises the pragmatist background of grounded theory much more, in particular by bringing the works of Charles Sanders Peirce more to the front as a fundament of a constructivist grounded theory. This concept is based on a relativist epistemology and understands methods as comparative and inductive. At the same time it takes the researchers' and participants' standpoints into account, and emphasizes reflexivity and pragmatism as a background (see also Charmaz and Bryant, 2010, p. 406).

In this context, the turn to **abduction** as a third way of making inferences beside induction and deduction becomes more relevant. Although Strauss used the term abduction in his writings very seldom, Bryant and Charmaz (2007a, p. 46) see abductive reasoning as characteristic of Strauss's thinking, as well as moving between induction and identifying surprising aspects in the data and explanations in developing the theory.

Abduction as a principle of discovery in grounded theory research

The idea of abduction has become quite prominent in the recent grounded theory discourse as a main principle of reasoning (see Strauss, 1987; Reichertz, 2007; Charmaz, 2014; Thornberg and Charmaz, 2014; Kennedy and Thornberg, 2018). Charmaz explains that grounded theory is an abductive method because it 'relies on *reasoning – making inferences* – about empirical experience' (2014, p. 201). Abduction was originally introduced by the pragmatist Charles Sanders Peirce (1878/1958) as a third principle of reasoning in addition to induction and deduction. Given the debates in grounded theory between the Glaserian approach (which strongly emphasizes a more or less pure inductivism as a feature of grounded theory) and the

Strauss and Corbin approach (suggesting a combination of induction and deduction once their second step of **axial coding** has been reached – see Kelle, 2005; and Chapter 4), the appeal of abduction may also be to open up a way out of this debate. However, the price for this way out is the stronger emphasis on creativity and intuition in proceeding along this path of inquiry: 'In abduction, qualitative researchers use a selective and creative process to examine how the data support existing theories or **hypotheses** as well as how the data may call for modifications in existing understandings' (Kennedy and Thornberg, 2018).

The main advancement is the stronger focus on how the researcher, the research situation and methodological choices inform what is identified as relevant in the field and how this informs what the theory in the end includes and focuses on. This replaces the naïve inductivism in which phenomena were discovered and emerged if the researchers were only open enough. It emphasizes abduction as a third principle of reasoning which is 'a way of capturing the dialectical shuttling between the domain of observations and the domains of ideas' (Atkinson et al., 2003, p. 149).

Postmodernism and situational analysis

Adele Clarke has taken a different road to updating grounded theory methodology and research. Her update is based on a turn in epistemology to postmodern thinking and a shift in interests in the research, and finally in a twist in the aim of research. Clarke unfolds an extensive and exhaustive discussion (Clarke, 2005) of recent approaches from Foucault's **discourse analysis** to Latour's actor-network theory (2005) in designing her new approach. The implications of these reflections can be summarized in some new interests: in embodiment and situatedness of multiple knowledges, which can be analyzed in studying the situation of the phenomenon under study. A shift from 'simplifying normativities' to complexities, differences and heterogeneities leads to the aim of developing sensitizing concepts and theoretically integrated analyses instead of searching for formal theories. It also leads to the analysis and mapping of situations and (narrative, visual, and historical) discourses (see Clarke, 2005, p. 19). Some of the points Clarke has made refer to shifts in the research orientation (situatedness of multiple knowledges, situations as starting points, differentiation instead of unity as the aim). Other points refer to modifications in the main aim (from theory to sensitive concepts as outcomes of the research; defining a construct such as a 'situational map' as a tool for analyzing all sorts of phenomena; and the turn to discourses) of the research. Nevertheless, Clarke sees herself as still rooted and embedded in grounded theory traditions, and mainly Strauss's approach. She is also still seen as a major protagonist in the field of grounded theory. Her situational analysis is an independent research programme but also a part of the family of methods that characterize grounded theory research. Together with Charmaz's approach, Clarke and situational analysis keep grounded theory connected to more recent methodological developments.

DEVELOPING THEORY BETWEEN DISCOVERY AND CONSTRUCTION

The major shift in the recent progression of grounded theory methodology is from the mythical approach of discovery to the more reflexive approach of construction. The earlier versions expect the concepts, insights and theory to emerge from the data, and the data to emerge from being in the field. Methodological aspects and the researchers' part in this process are more or less neglected. It is important for the researchers to be open, and categories and the theory would find their way out of the phenomenon into the data and to the researcher. Induction is the key concept of this process. In the further progress of the methodology and in reaction to critiques, this process was enriched with methodological instruments (e.g. the coding paradigm) for elaborating the analysis of the data. The role of the researchers in the process was not much discussed, except for being distorted by too much theoretical knowledge, too much orientation on methods and the like. This summary is perhaps a bit exaggerated so as to demonstrate the difference of a model based on construction instead of discovery. Constructivist grounded theory emphasizes that researchers do not simply find insights in the field but actively search for them. Their interests, interpretations, tools and practices in the process influence and determine the research and its outcomes. These influences by the research and the researchers on the issue under study and the insights that are produced are no longer seen as a mistake, but recognized as something, which may be ignored but will nevertheless be at stake. Acknowledging these influences and thus the more recent understandings of research in general makes grounded theory research more reflexive and more adequate and up-to-date.

THE USE OF EXISTING LITERATURE IN GROUNDED THEORY RESEARCH

A major debate in the understanding of grounded theory research between pure discovery and reflexive construction was about how far researchers should read and use existing literature before and during their empirical work. This issue could be seen as a technical problem, but the debate has turned it into an epistemological concern. The whole debate goes back to Glaser and Strauss's suggestion: 'An effective strategy is, at first, literally to ignore the literature of theory and fact on the area under study' (1967, p. 37). Bryant and Charmaz (2007c, p. 19) show that this debate has been going on ever since. Glaser (1998, p. 67), for example, insists on staying away from doing a literature review about existing theories and research when starting a grounded theory study, and states that researchers should postpone the literature research until their grounded theory is nearly completed. In a similar purist way, Holton (2007, p. 269) sees the literature review as embedded in other aspects which might limit the researchers' openness to their field and that should therefore be avoided, such as a 'preconceived problem statement, interview protocols, or extensive review of literature'.

However, the decision for or against using existing literature goes beyond the theories about the issue under study, but can refer to several forms of literature in a qualitative study, including:

- theoretical literature about the topic of the study;
- empirical literature about earlier research in the field of the study or similar fields;
- methodological literature about how to do research and how to use the methods that are chosen;
- theoretical and empirical literature to contextualize, compare and generalize the findings.

There are a number of arguments to be raised against the original stance of Glaser and Strauss (1967), and those who later maintained and emphasized it, such as Holton or Glaser. First of all, at the time of Glaser and Strauss (1967), there were a lot of unresearched issues whose understanding could be obstructed by taking in too much literature beyond the issue and the field. In the meantime the range of (completely) unstudied issues has become smaller. Second, there is a lot of literature on the methodological level about how to do a grounded theory study, which might be helpful to know for conceiving your own study. The same is the case with the existing examples of applying this approach. Third, the position Glaser and Strauss expressed was formulated against their backgrounds of being experienced researchers in their field and not novices still early on their path to developing expertise about research and their field. If we compare the situation of Glaser and Strauss in the mid-1960s, after long experience of doing research, with PhD students nowadays trying to find their way into a field where greater or lesser amounts of research has already occurred, and into research in general, their needs might be different. Dunne (2011) started from being a PhD student doing a grounded theory study and reflected about the use of literature in grounded theory research more generally. His analysis includes five reasons why the original abstinence position (stay away from literature reviews) should be replaced by a reflected form of using literature in the study without giving up openness to the issue and field. A good literature review can help to develop a rationale and justification for a study and to contextualize it, to find out if the same study has already been accomplished, bring more clarity in the coding and theory development, and increase the researchers' sensitivity for what they are doing (see also Dunne, 2011, p. 116).

Thornberg (2012) has taken these reflections as a starting point for outlining his concept of an 'informed grounded theory'. He problematizes the issue of delaying a literature review in your study even more radically with arguments showing that researchers who do not read before and during their research are not up-to-date in their fields, lose knowledge, and risk doing atheoretical studies. Applications for funding, ethical reviews and acceptance on PhD programmes are based on demonstrating a command of the literature, and thus become difficult without it. Finally, researchers mostly are able to distinguish between the literature and their own findings in the field. Dunne concludes from reviewing the debate about this issue that there 'now appears to be a growing consensus that some middle ground must be reached' (2011, p. 117). This consensus integrates the claim of openness in grounded theory with the practical needs and advantages of early literature searches and reviews.

That you should not shy away from reading before and during your study seems absolutely appropriate if you only take into account the writings about grounded theory methodology. But there is plenty of research and scientific knowledge in almost every possible field of grounded theory research. Therefore, you should take the existing substantive literature into account but try to reflect where it begins to impose on your perception of the phenomena in the field in a restricting way.

WHAT DOES THEORY MEAN FOR DOING GROUNDED THEORY?

As discovering, developing or constructing theory are the major aims of grounded theory research, some reflections about its concept of theory might be helpful. Here we can distinguish between the general concept of theory behind this research from the outset and the concept of theory as an outcome product of the process. Glaser and Strauss (1967, p. 3) outlined their basic understanding of what 'theory' is about at the beginning of their book. This definition shows already the double character of theory in their understanding. They mention academic purposes, such as theoretical advances in sociology, to guide research and to give a perspective for understanding behaviour and data. At the same time they expect theories to be relevant in practical applications and helpful for the practitioners. This double character of theory has led to differing understandings later in the development of the methodologies of grounded theory. Glaser, for example, emphasizes the **relevance of research** for practitioners and lay people much more than for academic purposes. Corbin and Strauss are much more interested in remaining connected to the academic worlds.

As an outcome of their research approach, Glaser and Strauss distinguish two forms of theories to be developed. **Substantive theory** refers to 'a delimited problem in a particular area, such as family relationships, formal organizations, or education' (Charmaz, 2014, p. 344). In the study briefly presented in Case study 1.1, the developed substantial theory provided a model for explaining the interaction with and about dying patients among relatives, professionals and the patient. Substantive theory is distinguished from '**formal theory**', which is developed later in the process and is understood as based on more abstract and general concepts relevant for more than one substantial area. The focus is on showing links between these concepts. In the example in Case study 1.1, formal theory meant the (empirical) transfer of the substantive theory on interaction with and about patients about death and dying to similar fields of interaction with unequal distributions of knowledge about a fact.

WHEN TO USE GROUNDED THEORY RESEARCH?

First, grounded theory as a research approach is ideal for a field in which a problem exists for which an explanation (or sometimes a solution) is missing. It is furthermore ideal for an area in which not much research and theorizing has been done before, so that there is space left for new insights and perspectives to be developed. Such fields are more difficult to find now than they were in the 1960s, when Glaser and Strauss invented the approach, although a lot of details still remain to be understood and explained in areas where research has been done already.

Second, you should do grounded theory research if you have enough time to use the whole programme of the approach (or one of the versions) and not just for a quick and dirty analysis of some phenomenon.

Third, you should use it when you have some readiness for an empirical adventure and less expectation of an elaborate but fixed set of rules. Atkinson et al. see as the real potential of grounded theory 'a collective awareness of the heuristic value of developmental **research design**s [through **theoretical sampling**] and exploratory data analytic strategies, not a "system" for conducting and analyzing research' (2003, pp. 162–3).

PLAN OF THE BOOK

In this book, we have used this chapter to make some introductory remarks about grounded theory and develop a brief overview of doing grounded theory. The next chapter addresses doing grounded theory by introducing the components, elements and the understanding of the research process in context. The third chapter is about data collection in grounded theory, the methods and data you can use for developing a theory empirically. Chapter 4 tackles what often is seen as the core of grounded theory research, and presents the various versions of coding in grounded theory in a comparative perspective. Chapter 5 focuses on recent developments in data analysis in this context. Chapter 6 is concerned with what to do after collecting and analyzing the first data and when to stop. It addresses key concepts such as theoretical sampling, theoretical sorting and **theoretical saturation**. Chapter 7 takes two perspectives on the output of grounded theory research. It first addresses writing in and about the process and results of a study. Then it pursues the questions of how to assess the quality of a study and which **criteria** are suggested for this purpose. Chapter 8 is about how a stronger emphasis on research design in grounded theory (which has not been a big topic so far) can contribute to giving new researchers in this area an orientation on how to plan and do their research. Chapter 9 discusses **triangulation** with the intention to show how this concept can promote the systematic side of this approach. The last chapter introduces the concept of doing perspectivist grounded theory and rounds off the discussion in the preceding chapters. Finally, you will find a glossary which should be helpful for understanding the concepts introduced in this chapter and unfolded in more detail in the coming chapters. The terms which are entries in the glossary are printed in bold the first time they appear in the text.

KEY POINTS

- The various versions of grounded theory research that now exist side by side differ in their epistemological backgrounds.
- Constructionist grounded theory means to take the role of the researcher into account.
- Constructionist grounded theory is also an attempt at uniting the field again.
- Inference in grounded theory research shuttles between induction, deduction and abduction.
- It is no longer up-to-date to ignore existing literature and research.
- Grounded theory research is still most appropriate where (theoretical) knowledge about an issue or problem is missing.

■ FURTHER READING

These sources develop the issues of this chapter in more detail:

Bryant, A. and Charmaz, K. (eds) (2007) *The SAGE Handbook of Grounded Theory.* London: Sage.

Charmaz, K. (2014) *Constructing Grounded Theory: A Practical Guide through Qualitative Analysis*, 2nd ed. London: Sage.

Dunne, C. (2011) 'The place of the literature review in grounded research', *International Journal of Social Research Methodology*, 14, 111–24.

Gibbs, G.R. (2018) *Analyzing Qualitative Data* (Book 6 of *The SAGE Qualitative Research Kit*, 2nd ed.). London: Sage.

CHAPTER TWO

DOING GROUNDED THEORY
KEY COMPONENTS, PROCESS AND ELEMENTS

CONTENTS

After reading this chapter, you should have a first orientation about:

- the key components of the methodology;
- the process of doing grounded theory;
- the major elements in this process;
- the relation of process and elements; and
- the issues detailed in the following chapters of the book.

KEY COMPONENTS OF GROUNDED THEORY METHODOLOGY

Grounded theory *methodology* is relevant for qualitative research in several ways. It provides a number of tools for doing qualitative analysis, which are also used in other contexts – like the specific conceptualization of coding data and materials. However, these concepts of data analysis have been developed as part of an integrated conception of how to do qualitative research, which includes a specific conceptualization of the research process. Although grounded theory coding can be applied in other contexts, it will reveal its potential most fully when you use it in an integrated manner. The key components of the integrated version of grounded theory originally outlined by Glaser and Strauss (1967) include cycles and integration of data collection and analysis, theory development and return to data collection. **Constant comparative analysis** and theoretical sampling are other features, as is theoretical saturation of categories as a cut-off point. Emergence of theory and codes instead of formulating both *a priori*, and finally an outcome beyond pure description but allowing for explanation of issues under study are also seen as core components (see also Hood, 2007, and Box 2.1).

BOX 2.1 KEY COMPONENTS OF GROUNDED THEORY

1. A spiral of cycles of data collection, coding, analysis, writing, design, theoretical categorization and data collection.
2. The constant comparative analysis of cases with each other and to *theoretical categories* throughout each cycle.

3. A theoretical sampling process based upon categories developed from ongoing data analysis.
4. The size of sample is determined by the '*theoretical saturation*' of categories rather than by the need for demographic 'representativeness', or simply a lack of 'additional information' from new cases.
5. The resulting theory is developed inductively from data rather than tested by data, although the developing theory is continuously refined and checked by data.
6. Codes '*emerge*' from data and are not imposed *a priori* upon it.
7. The substantive and/or formal theory outlined in the final report takes into account all the variations in the data and conditions associated with these variations. The report is an *analytical product rather than a purely descriptive account. Theory development is the goal* (Hood, 2007, p. 154, original italics).

Over the years, grounded theory methodology has proliferated into several versions of how to do it, which are documented in a number of textbooks (e.g. Glaser and Strauss, 1967; Glaser, 1978; Strauss, 1987; Strauss and Corbin, 1990; Clarke, 2005; Charmaz, 2014; Corbin and Strauss, 2015; Holton and Walsh, 2017– see Chapter 1). These books take different starting points and present different approaches to grounded theory or elements in this methodology. New protagonists have entered the field – like Juliet Corbin or Kathy Charmaz, Tony Bryant or Judith Holton. Glaser (1992) has taken different stances and criticized the writings of Strauss and Corbin (1990). Charmaz and Bryant have taken a more constructivist approach to grounded theory research; Clarke has taken up debates about **postmodernism**. This includes reservations about the idea of discovering a theory in the field and the data, and about aiming at constructing theories that are grounded in the field and the data. The role of 'data' in the process has been discussed as well. Nevertheless, and despite the further development, proliferation and debates in the field in the last 40 years, the following aspects (see also Bryant and Charmaz, 2007c, p. 12; and Wiener, 2007) can be defined as integral for using grounded theory *methodology*:

- data gathering, analysis and construction proceed concurrently;
- coding starts with the first interview and/or **field notes**;
- **memo** writing also begins with the first interview and/or field notes;
- theoretical sampling is the disciplined search for patterns and variations;
- theoretical sorting of memos sets up the outline for writing the paper;
- theoretical saturation is the judgement of when there is no need to collect further data;
- a basic social process that accounts for most of the observed behaviour is identified.

This chapter gives a brief summary of doing grounded theory in a process-oriented perspective and spells out these integral aspects in more detail. The differences between the versions of doing grounded theory mainly refer to details in the ways of doing data collection (see Chapter 3) and analysis (see Chapters 4 and 5) and rather fundamental epistemological positions (see Chapter 1). The general consensus about how to understand the process of doing grounded theory and which basic elements it should include has not been broken. So in this chapter, we will proceed with a more integrated and not a version-specific presentation.

THE PROCESS OF DOING GROUNDED THEORY
Traditional concepts of research process

The conception of the research process developed by Glaser and Strauss (1967) in their grounded theory approach becomes clearer when it is contrasted to the traditional conception of the research process. The traditional version of quantitative social sciences ideally starts from theories and from building a model: before entering the field to be studied, and while still sitting at their desks, researchers construct a model of the assumed conditions and relations. The researchers' starting point is the theoretical knowledge taken from the literature or earlier empirical findings. From this, hypotheses are derived, which are then operationalized and tested against empirical conditions. The concrete or empirical 'objects' of research, like a certain field or real persons, have the status of the exemplary against which assumed general relations (in the form of hypotheses) are tested. The aim is to guarantee that your study is representative in its data and findings (e.g. because random samples of the persons that are studied are drawn). A further aim is to break down complex relations into distinct variables: this allows the researchers to isolate and test their effects. Theories and methods are prioritized over the object of the research. Theories are tested and perhaps falsified along the way. If they are enlarged, it is through additional hypotheses, which are again tested empirically, and so on. A main feature of this conceptualization of the research process includes that it can be broken down into steps, which are applied one after the other. In quantitative research, **sampling**, for example, comes first. Data collection only begins once the sample has been drawn and the potential participants have been identified. Data collection will be finished in most studies before the analysis of the data begins. Research is organized as a step by step process. Qualitative research is also often oriented on such a step by step logic, but the understanding of process in grounded theory research challenges such a logic.

The research process in grounded theory research

In contrast to the above theory-driven and linear model of the research process, groun-ded theory research prioritizes the data and the field under study over theoretical assumptions. Accordingly, theories should not be applied to the subject being studied but are 'discovered' and formulated in working with the field and the empirical data to be found in it. People or materials to be studied are selected according to their relevance to the research topic: they are not selected to construct a (statistically) representative sample of a general population. The aim is not to reduce complexity by breaking it down into variables: rather it is to increase complexity by including context. Methods also have to be appropriate to the issue under study and have to be chosen accordingly.

What was outlined above as several steps applied one after the other is integrated in the process of grounded theory: the first data that are collected are immediately analyzed. The analysis and the questions it raises drive the sampling of the second case (group, **site**, situation, etc.). The new data are then immediately analyzed and compared to the first case. From then on, the collection, analysis and sampling pro-ceed in an integrated way aiming at developing the theory. Figure 2.1 displays this integrated (or circular) concept of research in the lower half of the figure in distinction to the traditional linear process in quantitative research.

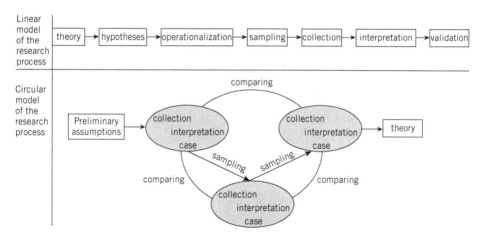

FIGURE 2.1 The circular research process in grounded theory as opposed to the traditional linear process

Source: Flick, 2014, p. 90

The attitude towards empirical work and data in this type of research can be out-lined as follows: 'The **principle of openness** implies that the theoretical structuring of the issue under study is postponed until the structuring of the issue under study by the persons being studied has "emerged"' (Hoffmann-Riem, 1980, p. 343). In grounded theory methodology it is often postulated (e.g. Glaser, 1978) that research-ers should at least suspend whatever *a priori* theoretical knowledge they bring into the field. However (in contrast to a widespread misunderstanding), this is postulated above mostly for the way to treat hypotheses and less for the decision concerning the research question. 'The delay in structuring implies the abandonment of the *ex ante* formulation of hypotheses. In fact, the research question is outlined under theoretical aspects' (Hofmann-Riem, 1980, p. 345)

ELEMENTS IN THE PROCESS OF DOING GROUNDED THEORY

Despite the emphasis on the integrated character of grounded theory research and methodology, it will be helpful to look at the elements of this process in some detail next, before some of these elements are discussed in a more extensive way in the following chapters.

Starting with a relevant problem: discovering or constructing it

As in other types of research, several possible starting points for doing a grounded theory study can be identified. A first starting point can be the researchers' curiosity, which made them select something as a research problem for developing a grounded theory. An example, given by Charmaz (2014), is her curiosity about how the pro-cess of recovering from addiction without treatment works. A personal experience or concern can be a second motivation. This was the case in Glaser and Strauss (1965a) when the researchers' experience with how their parents' dying was 'managed' in hospitals made them study this process (see Chapter 1, Case study 1.1). Gaps in the state of a scientific field can be a third point of departure based on research questions resulting from earlier research, the lack of theoretical models, theories, or explana-tions for a certain problem. The emergence of a new phenomenon or the discovery of a new problem can be a fourth reason for doing a grounded theory study – a new kind of chronic illness may suggest a study of the experience of people concerned with it. Or the relevance of a certain context (e.g. homelessness) for living with traditional forms of chronic illness may be identified as a research problem. In all these cases, researchers take a decision on what they want to study.

Identifying a research problem gives the issue a specific shape – certain aspects are more interesting, others are less prominent. To identify an issue as a topic for a grounded theory study entails a decision on a research perspective, aiming at developing a new theory, where so far theoretical knowledge has been lacking. It also includes conceiving the problem in such a way that it is worth being studied with a perspective aiming at theory (development) and then to construct a phenomenon as a specific research issue. Finally, it includes developing a research question (which aspects will be studied first or mainly, etc.). Although the initial research question can be revised and although the researcher might find out along the way what the most important aspects of an issue under study are, any grounded theory study should start with making a research question explicit.

These aspects of identifying an issue for research, and of giving it a specific shape, demonstrate that issues are not just discovered but are constructed in a specific way (see also Chapter 8).

Getting started: sensitizing concepts

Sensitizing concepts can be a good starting point. These are concepts that give the researcher a 'general sense of references and guidance in approaching empirical instances … suggest directions along which to look … and rest on a general sense of what is relevant' (Blumer, 1970, p. 58). They can be helpful as heuristic devices for giving researchers an orientation. Concepts such as 'trust', 'identity', and the like can be such starting points for identifying relevant problems and first conceptualizations in a field. Once a specific problem has been identified, for which empirical analysis and theoretical explanation are lacking, the next step will be to find contexts in which to begin to study it.

An example may illustrate this. Chronic illness of homeless adolescents is an issue, which is not very well analyzed empirically or theoretically. In our study concerning health practices of adolescents living on the streets in Germany (see Flick and Röhnsch, 2007), we came across several cases of adolescents reporting a more or less severe chronic illness, which made us start a project about this issue. The next question is where to find people in this situation more systematically: where would you meet potential participants for such a story, what kind of chronic illness would be most instructive as a starting point for developing a first understanding of this phenomenon, etc.? In this phase of the research, the identification of participants and contexts to begin with is not yet a question of sampling, but rather a question of discovery, exploration and creativity, and imagination. Sometimes it is necessary to ask experts, professionals, or colleagues for their suggestions about where to commence your research. Once this first case or first materials have been found, researchers should immediately begin to analyze it to advance their understanding of the issue.

Research ethics in grounded theory research

Research ethics have become more important for qualitative research in general (see Flick, 2018c). In grounded theory methodology they do not seem to be a big issue. *The SAGE Handbook of Grounded Theory* (Bryant and Charmaz, 2007b) and other recent textbooks (e.g. Charmaz, 2014) do not include specific chapters or a number of entries in the index for this topic. Books or chapters on research ethics do not often refer to grounded theory research as an example (e.g. Mauthner et al., 2002). At the same time, this issue becomes more relevant, when qualitative research has to be approved by ethics committees and has to meet ethical standards. Here again, a grounded theory study may face the expectation of a clear research design (see Chapter 8) which answers questions like: which methods will be applied, to whom, to how many people and why? This again may contradict a more open approach like grounded theory methodology, in which many of these questions can only be answered along the way in the research process. One example reflecting this problem is the discussion of the role of interview guides in Charmaz (2014) as a requirement produced by **institutional review board** assessments.

If theoretical sampling (see Chapter 6) is applied in a consistent way, research-ers will decide from the progress of the analysis, whom or which groups to include next in their sample. Again it may be helpful to construct a possible design – what do the researchers expect in the beginning of their project (when presenting it to the ethics committee); how many participants coming from which social groups or backgrounds do they expect to include, etc.? Trying to be as clear as possible in formulating a research question may be helpful here (see also Chapter 8).

Advancing in the field: from purposive to theoretical sampling

Sampling in grounded theory research is often linked to theoretical sampling and used as an alternative model to statistical sampling (see Chapter 6): 'Theoretical sampling ... means seeking and collecting pertinent data to elaborate and refine categories in your emerging theory' (Charmaz, 2014, p. 192). Charmaz distinguishes other forms of sampling often misunderstood as being theoretical sampling. The beginning of research is based on selection through 'initial sampling' or convenience sampling, which will allow you to get into the field and in touch with first cases and insights. Then you will go on with more purposeful strategies of sampling – directed at finding specific cases, a variation in the material and the like (see Chapter 6 for examples of such strategies). Theoretical sampling – in the strict meaning of the concept and according to more recent publications – will only start later in the process. It is focused more on finding cases, which will allow further development of the rudimentary theory and its categories developed so far.

Collecting or producing relevant data

Grounded theory methodology (literature) places a strong focus on two 'steps': sampling and analyzing data. There is less emphasis on how to turn phenomena into data in the process, which means that there is less advice on how to arrive at data to analyze once the fields or cases have been selected according to theoretical sampling. First of all, we find general statements like 'All is data' (Glaser, 2002). Looking at textbooks of grounded theory gives the impression that explicit methods of collecting data are covered less than how to analyze them. Then we find a, sometimes harsh, debate about the status of data (collection) in the process of developing a grounded theory. This debate oscillates between the notions that data emerge in the field (Glaser), that data are collected by using specific methods (Strauss, 1987), and that data are constructed or produced by the researcher in the field (see Charmaz, 2014). Beyond the epistemological differences in these notions, it seems obvious that researchers use methods for arriving at data. Grounded theory methodology is not linked to a preferable method for collecting or producing data.

However, the whole concept of the research process (see above) has been developed in projects based on **participant observation** (see Chapter 3), including more or less formalized conversations or interviews with members of the field (see Case study 1.1). This research strategy is based on repeated field contact and allows returning to the field to collect more data and to adapt data collection to the needs and questions resulting from the analysis of the data so far. Interview studies are in most cases based on meeting the interviewee once and often rely on an interview schedule for all interviewees.

If you want to make the most out of using grounded theory methodology, you should consider a strategy that can accommodate several forms of data (as in observation or in ethnography) rather than expecting to do only a limited number of interviews. Furthermore, the epistemological debates mentioned in Chapter 1 should not confuse you in accessing data: data do not emerge from a field and not everything *is* data. But almost everything can be used and turned into data – whatever is helpful to understand the process and the field the research is in and to answer the research questions. Then you can use different sorts of phenomena and materials and turn them into data (see Chapter 9). And you can use different methods to collect and document such materials as data. Whatever method you use in this step will influence what you see as data and how phenomena and materials appear as data. Thus, as in other kinds of research, the use of certain methods will produce data, which you can use for constructing a theory that is grounded in these data.

Analyzing data in the process

The analysis of data in grounded theory is described in detail in two later chapters (Chapters 4 and 5) in respect to the different versions that have been developed over the years. Here only some basics shall be mentioned. Analyzing data means to apply several forms of coding, starting from open coding to more structured and focused or selective forms. Coding means to develop categories, properties and relations among them. Coding is a process, which includes at least three steps (or ways of coding) with different aims. The starting point is always open coding, sometimes called **initial coding** (Charmaz, 2014). Later, some form of more structured coding is included. The ways of structuring this coding can vary between the approaches. This can be **theoretical coding** (Glaser, 1978), axial coding (Strauss and Corbin, 1990) or **focused coding** (Charmaz, 2014). **Selective coding** is the last step (Glaser, 1978, sees it as prior to theoretical coding), which means that data are scanned for more evidence for core categories, which are central to the developing theory. Coding aims to identify structures in the material – like core categories (Strauss), basic social processes (Glaser), or story lines (Strauss and Corbin).

The different ways of coding should not be seen in a one after the other logic. Rather the researcher will return to open coding, if the other forms of coding raise questions only to be answered by developing new categories. The endpoint of coding is theoretical saturation – when continuing coding or the integration of new data would not lead to new theoretical insights (see Chapter 6). Varying emphasis is placed on theoretical sorting, the organizing of codes and material around a developing structure. In the classic studies at least (Glaser and Strauss, 1965a, for example), coding related to the phenomenon under study leads to a substantive grounded theory first. Coding, analyzing and collecting data can be continued to the stage of developing a formal grounded theory (Glaser, 2007b), which is relevant also beyond the phenomenon and fields that were studied originally. For example, Glaser and Strauss (1965a) have developed a substantive grounded theory about the interaction happening (or missing) around the dying of patients (between relatives of the patient and staff in a hospital, or the patient and relatives and staff). A main result was interaction strategies used for receiving more information about the patient's situation from the staff, for example. This was then extended empirically to other situations of interaction where one party holds information the other party does not have but would like to have (examples were situations of buying/selling a used car) to develop a formal theory of negotiations. Many of the applications of the grounded theory methodology, however, concentrate on describing and analyzing the phenomenon they study; some of them really end up providing a theory built around a core category, for example, and only few arrive at developing their findings further into a formal theory.

Writing in the process

Another essential of the research process in grounded theory is the emphasis on writing, and in particular on writing memos throughout all the stages (see Lempert, 2007; Gibbs, 2018; and Chapter 7). The memos should document the process of accessing the field, working in it, and developing and defining categories from the material and bits and pieces of the developing theory. The theory is then based on sorting and developing the memos, which are also seen as a contribution to writing about the research in a report or publication. Continuously writing about the research, advances and steps back, is also seen as a prerequisite for reflexivity about the research, participants, data, findings and outcomes.

CASE STUDY 2.1 AWARENESS OF DYING AND AWARENESS CONTEXTS

Glaser and Strauss developed grounded theory as a method in their study (see also Case study 1.1) on the handling of death and dying in hospitals (Glaser and Strauss, 1965a). Their research question was on what interacting with dying people depends upon, and how the knowledge of a person's imminent death determines the interaction with him or her. More concretely, what they studied were the forms of interaction between the dying person and the clinical staff of the hospital, between the staff and the relatives, and between the relatives and the dying person. Which tactics are applied in the contact with dying people, and what part does the hospital play as a social organization here?

The central concept at the end of the analysis was 'awareness contexts'. This concept expresses what each of the interactants knows about a certain state of the patient and what he or she assumes about the other interactants' awareness of his or her own knowledge. This awareness context may change due to the patient's situation or due to new information for one or all of the participants.

Four types of awareness were found. *Closed awareness* means the patients do not suspect their approaching death. *Suspicion awareness* means they have a suspicion concerning this issue. *Awareness of mutual pretence* is the case when everybody knows, but nobody says it openly. *Open awareness* is when the patients know about their situation and speak frankly about it with all the others.

More generally, the analysis of awareness contexts included their description and the precondition of a social structure in each context (social relations, etc.). It also comprised resulting interactions, which included the tactics and counter-tactics of the participants in order to bring about changes in the awareness context and also the consequences of each form of interaction for those who are involved, for the hospital, and for further interactions. The analysis was elaborated to a theory of awareness contexts through comparisons with other situations of mutual pretence and differing awareness of those who are involved, into which this typology fits. As examples, the authors mention buying and selling cars or 'clowning at the circuses' (1965a, p. 277), and so on. Integrating such other fields and the grounded theories developed for them formulates a formal theory of awareness.

All in all, this very early research example allows us to follow the steps of grounded theory development based on one central concept. The study is not only instructive from a methodological point of view but was very influential in the sociology of illness and dying and in areas such as nursing, for example.

CONCLUSION: PROCESS OR ELEMENTS

In this chapter, you should have received a first orientation about the research programme of grounded theory and the process of research which is characteristic of it. Before the elements of this process are discussed in more detail in the following chapters, some concluding remarks are in order. The whole approach, first, is strongly based on an integrated understanding of the research. This means that it is, in principle, possible to take single elements out of the whole and to use them in other approaches – for example, just to apply the method used for data analysis in a different context. However, the whole approach was constructed based on using theoretical sampling (see Chapter 6), constant comparison of data (see Chapter 4) and the development of theories via theoretical saturation (see Chapter 6) – which Hood calls the 'Troublesome Trinity' but at the same time complains that only few researchers and studies have used this trinity correctly (Hood, 2007, p. 163). Second, given the lively debate in the field about the 'right' way of doing grounded theory (see Chapters 1, 5 and 6) the consensus about the process and elements outlined here is rather strong, and differences refer more to the 'how to do' in the elements (e.g. forms of coding). Therefore, in some of the following chapters the differences will be discussed and outlined for each of the most prominent approaches. Third, to nail down the process into steps will undervalue the integrated character of the whole approach. Thus, the presentation of elements, as in this chapter, tries to avoid such a step by step understanding and aims at outlining these elements in their main aspects.

● KEY POINTS

- Grounded theory was originally an integrated concept of research and process.
- Elements can be discussed analytically on their own, but the whole process should be kept in mind.
- Elements can be taken out and used separately but that will distort the overall logic (and power) of grounded theory research.

■ FURTHER READING

The outline of grounded theory elements in this chapter is filled out in more detail in the following sources:

Charmaz, K. (2014) *Constructing Grounded Theory: A Practical Guide through Qualitative Analysis*. London: Sage.

Gibbs, G.R. (2018) *Analyzing Qualitative Data* (Book 6 of *The SAGE Qualitative Research Kit*, 2nd ed.). London: Sage.

Hood, J. (2007) 'Orthodoxy versus power: the defining traits of grounded theory', in A. Bryant and K. Charmaz (eds), *The SAGE Handbook of Grounded Theory*. London: Sage, pp. 151–64.

Thornberg, R. and Charmaz, K. (2014) 'Grounded theory and theoretical coding', in U. Flick (ed.), *The SAGE Handbook of Qualitative Data Analysis*. London: Sage, pp. 153–69.

CHAPTER THREE

GETTING IN

DATA COLLECTION IN GROUNDED THEORY

CONTENTS

CHAPTER OBJECTIVES

After reading this chapter, you should understand:

- the role of data in the various versions of grounded theory research;
- the major forms of data collection in grounded theory research;
- problems linked to several kinds of data in grounded theory research; and
- more about how to use the major methods of data collection in grounded theory research.

In this chapter, we first look at the ways the five versions of grounded theory research address data collection and what advice they provide for collecting your own data. Issues are the role of data and of methods for collecting data. In the second part of the chapter, we will turn the perspective around and look at some of the major approaches for data collection available and how they can be used in grounded theory, and also for advancing the practicability of grounded theory research for novices in qualitative or grounded theory research.

THE ORIGINAL APPROACH OF GLASER AND STRAUSS

The focus in the methodological literature on grounded theory research was always more on how to analyze materials collected in one way or another. Glaser and Strauss (1967, p. 161) underline in their chapter on new sources for qualitative data, that they basically had two kinds of data in mind. They refer regularly to documents as data and use the term 'caches of documents' (e.g. p. 167), where the researchers can identify and discover new reserves of data. The second kind of data they discuss comes from fieldwork. Glaser and Strauss also stress the similarities between fieldwork and documents – for example, collected in library work, where sources have to be discovered and then analyzed and compared. Both approaches to data are rather open in their format – imagination and discovery direct the collection of data and then the ways they are compared and analyzed. More strongly formatted methods of collecting data, such as interviews, do not play a major role in this context, although Glaser and Strauss suggest seeing and treating caches of documents similarly to interviews (1967, p. 167). Why is this (limited) focus in Glaser and Strauss's original writings interesting? It gives some support to the thesis that the original version of grounded theory research was very much focused on materials which are rather open in their format. The main method of collecting data was to discover materials to which the researchers could easily and repeatedly return. Whereas the standard set-ting in studies with interviews (or focus groups) is based on single meetings with the participant(s), fieldwork (participant observation and ethnography) is based on the researchers' longer presence in the field where observations and conversations can be continued. In such a setting, constant comparison as well as theoretical sampling can be much more easily integrated into the process of data collection and vice versa. Applying these two steps for clarifying new insights from the analysis in an interview study requires returning to the interviewee (which is quite unusual) or to continue with a 'new' interview/ee. Accordingly, neither *Awareness of Dying* (Glaser and Strauss, 1965a) nor *The Discovery of Grounded Theory* (Glaser and Strauss, 1967) include much reference to interviews or to individuals as cases.

Theoretical sampling as data collection

In the definition of one of their major concepts, Glaser and Strauss also outline the role of data collection: 'theoretical sampling is the process of data collection' (1967, p. 45). Data collection and methods for this purpose mainly become relevant in the context of theoretical sampling, as Glaser and Strauss underline in their description of the research process: 'theoretical sampling usually requires reading documents, interviewing, and observing at the same time, since all slices of data are relevant. There is little, if any, systematic interviewing of a sample of respondent' (1967, p. 75).

Glaser and Strauss here demonstrate their preference for an integrated approach to data collection, which is not based on a single method or a methodologically elaborate form of data collection. Where single methods are an issue, observation or ethnog-raphy is their choice. Talking to participants in a more formal way – a specific type of interview, for example – only becomes relevant in the context of observation. At the same time, collecting **verbal data** is basically driven by the analysis and theory development, as they clearly state (1967, pp. 75–6). Interviews become shorter the more the study advances and are used to 'ask direct questions bearing on ... categories' (1967, pp. 75–6). This demonstrates a somewhat pragmatic use of interviews as a tool for providing missing information rather than a systematic database for comparisons, and resulting from a comparable way of data production. The idea is more to find or discover data than to produce them in a systematic way. How long interviews will last, how comprehensive they should be or how many interviews should be done at the same time depends on the state of the analysis and theory development. Whether or not the approaches used in data collection are appropriate can only be judged in retrospect (in the light of the theory that resulted) but hardly in planning the research.

LATER WORKS OF STRAUSS AND CORBIN

This treatment of the issues of data, collection of data and methods of data collection is continued in the later development of Strauss' work (1987) and in collaboration with Juliet Corbin (Strauss and Corbin, 1990, 1994). Here again, the focus of the methodological elaboration of the approach is on analyzing (all sorts of data) and developing a theory from the analysis. Data collection is basically referred to as a problem of theoretical sampling – which provides cases, incidents, or documents to select, but not so much how to collect them as data. In the current edition of their collaborative book (Corbin and Strauss, 2015), we find a greater recognition of methods of data collection. Again, it is emphasized that grounded theory research uses 'many different sources of data' (p. 37), but then interviews and observations are discussed in a bit more detail. This discussion can be characterized in two ways. First, a brief and general overview of interviews, for example, is given, distinguishing unstructured interviews, **semi-structured interview**s, and structured interviews. The summary of interviews is very generally based on literature about qualitative research and not specifically for their use in grounded theory research. The second characterization is that practical, technical and planning issues are mainly regarded as relevant because institutional review boards (IRBs) ask for the use and presentation of interviews and observational guides 'even in grounded theory studies' (2015, p. 43). The major focus in presenting grounded theory research remains on data analysis and is mainly extended by (new) ways of presenting the findings.

GLASER AND CLASSICAL GROUNDED THEORY

Glaser (2001) takes a specific stance about the role of data collection, in particular in critical distinction from Corbin and Strauss. On the one hand, he holds 'All is data', which expresses the idea that grounded theory research is not about using specific forms of data nor is it tied to any particular method of data collection. On the other hand, he makes a clear distinction between grounded theory research and qualitative data analysis (or qualitative research in general). For Glaser, the latter is limited to description and preconceptions of data collection as with specific methods, whereas grounded theory research heads for theory development and thus explanation without such a preconception. Finally, Glaser does not limit his approach to qualitative data, but has always argued for using quantitative data in grounded theory research if that is helpful (e.g. Glaser and Strauss, 1967, Chapter 8; Glaser, 1978). In his own first comprehensive outline of the approach (Glaser, 1978) data collection is treated as a part of theoretical sampling again (1978, pp. 44–54). Glaser describes a process starting from 'initial decisions ... based only on a sociological perspective and on a problem area' (p. 44). According to this concept research is driven by an interest in a field and the immediate search for conceptualization. Data are just a means for supporting this conceptualization, but they are not seen as linked to the systematic use of methods, for example. *'The researcher in this mode does not have to know beforehand*, he has to believe his data and theoretically sample for it' (1978, p. 45). Glaser then sees the researcher confronted with the problem that the 'analyst may feel that his [sic] non-preconceived field yields only scattered observation' (1978, p. 46). The major question then is 'Where next?' (1978, p. 46) for other incidents, participants or groups. In this context Glaser discusses briefly what to do when the 'feeling of theoretical saturation emerges while in the field' (p. 53) which often is discovered to be a false sense, when data are analyzed in more detail. Finally, Glaser addresses issues of secondary analysis, which here is understood as analyzing one's own data, originally collected for other purposes, again for the current study. Later, Glaser (with Holton, 2004) states about the use of data in grounded theory research, that it neither requires specific forms of interview, nor 'tape-recorded data' but that field notes are preferred (2004, p. 26).

More recent outlines of classic grounded theory (Holton and Walsh, 2017) discuss the issue of where the data come from as 'finding your data', for which all kinds of data can be relevant. The major tasks for researchers are to gain access to the field, to take notes about what can be seen and what is said, to integrate the collection and analysis in the fieldwork and 'not to undermine the discovery of latent patterns in data by preconceiving what to look for or what type of data to use' (2017, p. 73).

In the further development of their originally collaborative writings Glaser and Strauss took and suggested differing paths to developing grounded theories. While Glaser insists on the distinctiveness of his approach from what Strauss (and Corbin) later suggests as methodology but also from the more general concepts of qualitative research, Strauss and Corbin outlined a more pragmatic use of methods and principles from the wider discussions. The divide between the two 'fathers' of grounded theory has motivated several members of the 'second generation' (see Morse et al., 2009) to develop new approaches and new attitudes to using methods of data collection in grounded theory research.

DATA COLLECTION IN SITUATIONAL ANALYSIS

For her approach of situational analysis as a further development of grounded theory research, Clarke (2005) expresses scepticism about the original understanding of the role of data in grounded theory research when she challenges the ways in which Glaser and Strauss originally referred to data in a quasi-magical and sacred way. In particular she rejects the idea of 'letting the data speak for themselves' (2005, p. 75).

Clarke takes up an essential aspect of how data collection is addressed in the earlier versions of grounded theory. In the original outlines of grounded theory research, theoretical insights in general and categories in a technical sense 'emerge' from the data if the researchers are only open enough in the field (and not 'disoriented' by taking existing theories and furthermore specific methods of data collection into account). Clarke's response to this idea is that researchers should collect data that are relevant for the situation under study, because: 'Awaiting "emergence" from the data is not enough' (2005, pp. 75–6).

Clarke discusses several forms of situational analysis from the angle of which kind of data should be collected. For the analysis of existing social worlds, Clarke sees interviews, organizational documents, archive data, observations and secondary data as relevant and also extends situational analysis to a multi-site/multiscape approach. Then she is interested in 'scapes' such as ethnoscapes (heterogeneous landscapes of persons, identities, etc.), mediascapes (from print and TV information), technoscapes (worlds and communications produced in and by devices), financescapes (investments and financial flows), and ideoscapes (images and ideologies) (pp. 165–6). Clarke also uses methods of discourse analysis (p. 174), and discourse data for the specific approaches of situational analysis, and in particular visual data for analyzing visual discourses (pp. 223–4; see also Rapley, 2018).

These brief remarks show that Clarke has a more explicit idea of how to design studies and, in particular, of how to use specific kinds of data for which purpose, and finally of how to collect them. As she states in the prologue of her book, her suggestions are less an alternative programme to grounded theory research in general, but an attempt 'to push grounded theory more fully around the postmodern turn through a new approach to analysis within the grounded theory framework' (2005, p. xxi).

CONSTRUCTIVIST GROUNDED THEORY

The most prominent version in grounded theory research is Charmaz's (2014) constructivist grounded theory. Charmaz not only revises a number of epistemological and methodological assumptions of early grounded theory, but takes a specific stance on data and data collection, although this remains in the methodological tradition that 'our data collection methods flow from the research question and where we go with it' (Charmaz, 2014, p. 27). Charmaz, however, takes a much more tool-oriented approach to methods: 'Just as the methods we choose influence what we see, what we bring to the study also influences what we *can* see' (2014, p. 27). For her, grounded theory research is not only a combination of theoretical sampling and the specific form of analysis, but provides a framework for other steps in the research process as well. She suggests using or developing methods in this framework, which are most promising for progressing with ideas and concepts. Her understanding of the role of data is driven by the problem under study, which should determine which methods to use for data collection and also which kinds of data should be used.

With these emphases, Charmaz is much more connected with the general methodological discussions in qualitative research. This connectedness overcomes the distinctions Glaser makes between grounded theory and qualitative research. In addition, she is closer to Clarke's openness, who also notes that whatever method is requested by the research problem should be used. However, Charmaz remains in the tradition of Glaser and Strauss when she discusses single methods for data collection in grounded theory research in more detail. She begins with ethnography and the analysis of documents (similarly to Glaser and Strauss, 1967) before she shifts the focus to interviewing.

Grounded theory as an ethnographic approach

The link between ethnography and grounded theory is double sided. Charmaz and Mitchell (2001) discuss how you can use grounded theory principles and methods in ethnography with the aim of providing solutions to problems in ethnographic research. They mention too many unfocused data, low-level description of all and nothing and lists of unintegrated categories (2001, p. 161). Solutions offered come from using theoretical sampling and coding procedures from grounded theory in ethnography and from aiming beyond mere descriptions. Charmaz (2014) also discusses ethnography as a method in grounded theory research and outlines the differences from other forms of ethnography, which focus more on describing settings and not so much on the issues or process, which is the aim of grounded theory ethnography. Another feature of using ethnography in grounded theory research is the transfer of the 'coding-in-collecting' approach usually applied in grounded theory research, comparing data with each other and with emerging categories during data collection (2014, p. 41).

Both suggestions aim at using ethnography for theory development about a phenomenon and not just for descriptions of a field. For this purpose, ethnography is reduced here from a comprehensive research attitude to a methodological tool for collecting data in the field.

Using documents

As the second type of data to be collected for constructivist grounded theory research, Charmaz suggests the use of either *elicited* or *extant* documents. The former include, for example, diaries, notes, and other texts produced for the research, whereas the latter have been produced for other purposes and are only selected by the researcher for the study. Here again, Charmaz follows Glaser and Strauss (1967), but links her suggestions more directly to the general methodological discourse in qualitative research about using documents – for example, in Coffey (2014). Both strategies (ethnography and the use of documents) are ways to gather 'rich data' in grounded theory research.

Intensive interviewing in constructivist grounded theory research

The major step forward in Charmaz's (2014) approach to data collection is her emphasis on using interviews, which she unfolds in greater detail in two chapters. For using interviews, she goes beyond Corbin and Strauss (2015) who only refer to the existence of several forms of more or less structured interviews (see above). Charmaz suggests her own form, intensive interviewing, which is described as 'a gently-guided, one-sided conversation that explores research participants' perspective on their personal experience with the research topic' (2014, p. 56; see Box 3.1).

BOX 3.1   KEY CHARACTERISTICS OF INTENSIVE INTERVIEWING

- Selection of research participants who have first-hand experience that fits the research topic.
- In-depth exploration of participants' experience and situations.
- Reliance on open-ended questions.
- Objective of obtaining detailed responses.
- Emphasis on understanding the research participant's perspective, meanings, and experience.
- Practice of following up on unanticipated areas of inquiry, hints, and implicit views and accounts of actions.

(Charmaz, 2014, p. 56)

The new term demonstrates that this form of interviewing is distinct from 'just doing interviews' as in other contexts of qualitative research. It is a form of interviewing which goes beyond what interviews or conversations meant in earlier versions of grounded theory research (mainly spontaneous, rather unformatted exchanges as a part of fieldwork and observations). And finally, this form of interview is more characterized by an attitude than by more or less explicit rules or specific types of questions and their sequence.

Charmaz suggests working with interview guides for two reasons mainly. The first is to give researchers an orientation in the field and in the situation of data collection. The second reason is less aimed at internal needs of doing the research but comes from the external context of legitimating the research. Similar to Corbin and Strauss, Charmaz points out that the expectations of IRBs are a major point of reference for developing a detailed interview guide (2014, p. 66). Nevertheless, Charmaz suggests that the interview guide should be developed, used and adapted according to the experiences in the process.

SUGGESTIONS FOR COLLECTING DATA IN GROUNDED THEORY RESEARCH: CONCLUSIONS

The different versions of grounded theory research discuss data collection in different ways. First, the range of suggestions stretches from rather indefinite concepts ('All is data' – Glaser) to finding data occasionally and in a rather open but unsystematic way (classic grounded theory research). Second, we also find suggestions extending from all sorts of data (slices of data – Glaser and Strauss) to be used in a very pragmatic way to loose references to existing methods (e.g. interviewing – Corbin and Strauss). Third, we find references to specific methods (such as discourse analysis or visual methods) depending on the concrete research question or situation/arena to be studied (Clarke), and a stronger reliance on a concept of interviewing which remains rather focused on the attitude to bring to encounters with participants and less on how to do (intensive) interviews. All these suggestions make sense from the perspective of experienced researchers looking back on a study and assessing whether it was appropriate to proceed the way in which they produced and used their data for developing a theory or analyzing a situation. At the same time, they leave researchers starting with their project (or research in general) with a rather vaguely defined toolkit and little guidance about which method to choose for their study and how to do their research with a particular method.

BEYOND INTUITION: DOING DATA COLLECTION IN GROUNDED THEORY

In what follows some of the methods that can be or are used in grounded theory research will be discussed to elaborate their orienting potential in a more systematic way (for overviews and more detail, see Flick, 2018d). The idea behind these considerations is that the outlines of methods to use for data collection in grounded theory textbooks often remain rather vague. They strongly appeal to the researchers' intuition in the fieldwork when it comes to how to do grounded theory research. To give you more orientation, some of the current discussions in the wider field of qualitative research on this how-to-do level (see also Flick, 2014, 2018c) will be integrated into the grounded theory research discourse.

Doing observations and ethnography in grounded theory research

The methodological discussion about observation and ethnography in qualitative research in general has some similarities to that about grounded theory research. Doing ethnography in particular can be understood in three ways. (1) As an *attitude* towards and in a field. Then the researchers take an open approach to what they study (with whatever method) and strongly focus on writing about what they experienced in the field (see for, example, Gubrium and Holstein, 2014). (2) As a strategy, i.e. as a methodological framework for applying a wider range of methods (e.g. observation, several forms of systematic interviewing and the analysis of documents). (3) As a specific method, i.e. as the methodological approach of a study mainly focused on observation in the field with some integrated conversations with its members. In particular, the first understanding was the background for developing the research programme of grounded theory in the beginning. The third understanding has led to a number of suggestions for how to do ethnography (see in particular Coffey, 2018; and Buscatto, 2018, for recent overviews), which might be a helpful orientation for grounded theory research.

One crucial challenge is to identify settings and situations to begin observations for an ethnography and the process of theoretical sampling, and where to find relevant events for further developing categories and the theory. Here, the suggestions by Spradley (1980) may give an orientation: social situations generally can be described along nine dimensions for observational purposes – space, actor, activity, object, act, event, time, goal, feeling (1980, p. 78).

As we saw above, Charmaz sees a difference between ethnography in general and in grounded theory research, that in the latter the focus is less on describing the setting than on the phenomenon or process that is studied. As both – setting as context, and phenomenon as main focus – depend on each other, it might be helpful to see the use of ethnography in grounded theory research as a process of identifying and focusing the phenomenon in the setting. How to arrive at such a focus in participant observation, for example, can either be an issue for the researchers' intuition – the ethnographic inspiration according to Gubrium and Holstein (2014). Or it can be understood as a process of several steps according to Spradley (1980, p. 34), who distinguishes three phases of participant observation. He suggests beginning with *descriptive observation* for an orientation in the field and for developing research questions. This should be followed by *focused observation* for narrowing the perspective on the relevant issues. The last phase is *selective observation*, and means to look for more evidence and examples.

These phases allow us to structure the process of observation. They are also oriented on the phases of the coding process in grounded theory. LeCompte and Schensul see research designs as relevant to research in ethnography: 'All good ethnographers try to create an overall design in which anticipated details and activities are spelled out as far as current information permits' (1999, p. 98; see also Chapter 8 and Coffey, 2018). Finally, Buscatto's (2018) discussion of reflexivity in the ethnographic research process can be helpful for sharpening the focus of the study and in collecting data.

Ethnography was the general framework for developing the methodology of grounded theory. At the same time, it was something grounded theorists wanted to surpass by going beyond mere description to theoretical explanation of problems and processes. Ethnographic approaches are still often used in grounded theory research. Some of the suggestions for how to do ethnography formulated in other research contexts can contribute to doing grounded theory ethnography in a more fruitful way.

Using interviews and narratives in grounded theory research

As the brief overview in the first part of the chapter has shown, interviews (as a method) are not very prominent in the methodological literature of grounded theory, except in Charmaz's version. It should also have become evident that the attitude to interviewing (as a gentle conversation) more than concrete suggestions for how to do interviews in a systematic way is the focus. If the intended constant comparison focuses on participants' subjective experiences, for example, and on comparing them in a more systematic way, it might be helpful to have interviews produced under rather similar conditions. The general attitudes to doing interviews are distinguished by Brinkmann and Kvale (2018, p. 19–20) with the two metaphors of the interviewer as a data miner or as a traveller. The concept of the data miner is closer to the original idea of discovery and emergence of concepts and theories in the field through empirical analysis (as in Glaser and Strauss, 1967), which unearths the core of a theoretical concept in the material. The second metaphor of the interview traveller sees interviewing (and research) more as a co-constructive process between participants and researchers based on interpretations. There are basically two ways of working with interviews: semi-structured interviews, and narrative and episodic interviews (see also Flick, 2014).

Semi-structured interviews

These are based on an interview guide consisting of a number of questions to be answered. Here the major challenges are to formulate adequate questions and to use the guide in an appropriately flexible way in the field. Brinkmann and Kvale (2018) suggest seven stages of interview research, which include *thematizing* as a formulation of the purpose of the study, designing the study and the interview, and doing the interview 'based on an interview guide and with a reflective approach'. There are helpful suggestions in the literature for how to work with such a format (see Roulston, 2014; and Roulston and Choi, 2018, for example) in general. We can also find more concrete suggestions for how to use this format with specific target groups – such as experts (Bogner et al., 2018) or children, for example (see MacDougall and Darbyshire, 2018).

Setting the stage for interviewing: For shaping the situation when doing interviews, Hermanns has outlined a number of stage directions for interviewing (2004, pp. 212–13), which include matters such as: how to explain to the interviewees what is expected from them during the interview; how to create a good atmosphere in the interview; and how to give room to allow interviewees to open up. Most crucial in these suggestions is that during the interview the researcher should try to discover not (existing) theoretical concepts, but rather the life world of the interviewee. Of similar importance is be aware that research questions are not the same as interview questions and to try to use everyday language instead of scientific concepts in the questions. Discovering theoretical concepts and using scientific concepts is something for the data analysis process: using concrete everyday wordings is what, in contrast, should happen in the questions and the interview.

Brinkmann and Kvale (2018, p. 62) add a number of suggestions for creating a good atmosphere in the interview. They also give detailed advice for how to translate research questions into interview questions (2018, p. 66).

Finally, Ulrich (1999) has suggested a number of key points for evaluating questions in interviews, which address the wording, the meaning, the relevance and position of individual questions in interview schedules (see Box 3.2).

BOX 3.2   KEY POINTS FOR EVALUATING QUESTIONS IN INTERVIEWS

1   Why do you ask this specific question?
    – What is its theoretical relevance?
    – What is the link to the research question?

2   For what reason do you ask this question?
    – What is the substantial dimension of this question?

3   Why did you formulate the question in this way (and not differently)?
    – Is the question easy to understand?
    – Is the question unambiguous?
    – Is the question productive?

4   Why did you position this question (or block of questions) at this specific place in the interview guide?
    – How does it fit into the rough and detailed structure of the interview guide?
    – How is the distribution of types of question spread across the interview guide?
    – What is the relation between single questions?

(Ulrich, 1999)

Narrative and episodic interviews

The second approach for using interviews is to rely more or mainly on narratives. In a period when he was in regular collaboration with Anselm Strauss, Fritz Schütze, in Germany, developed a specific method of narrative interviewing (see Riemann and Schütze, 1987; Rosenthal, 2004). Here the interviewee tells 'the story of the area of interest in question as a consistent story of all relevant events from its beginning to its end' (Hermanns, 1995, p. 183). This method is mainly used in biographical research,

BRESCIA UNIVERSITY
COLLEGE LIBRARY

sometimes also with the aim of developing a theory from analyzing a number of such interviews. The main methodological element is the generative narrative question ('I want to ask you to tell me how the story of your life occurred ' – Hermanns, 1995, p. 182 – see Box 3.3 for an example).

BOX 3.3   EXAMPLE OF A GENERATIVE NARRATIVE QUESTION

I want to ask you to tell me how the story of your life occurred. The best way to do this would be for you to start from your birth, with the little child that you once were, and then tell all the things that happened one after the other until today. You can take your time in doing this, and also give details, because for me everything is of interest that is important for you.

(Hermanns, 1995, p. 182)

When this works, the interviewees will begin and unfold a story (of their lives or the area that is the focus of the study). It is important that the interviewer does not interrupt the informants in their narrations and postpones questions (for better comprehension, theoretical issues, etc.) to after the end of the narration. The methodological assumption behind the method is that in an uninterrupted narrative, interviewees mention more details and embarrassing or delicate issues than in other (question–answer-oriented) interviews. Then the methods provide the rich data a grounded theory study into a process or biographical research question will need. The concept and theory development is mainly concentrated on the analysis of the data.

Whereas the **narrative interview** provides rather tour d'horizon narratives (of life histories, for example), sometimes small-scale narratives (Bamberg, 2012) are more relevant and easier to handle in a (grounded theory) study. For this purpose, the **episodic interview** (see Flick, 2014, Chapter 18; and Flick, 2018a, Chapter 3) may be more adequate. It comprises a combination of questions (e.g. 'What is health for you, what do you link to that word?') and invitations to recount situations ('episodes') in which specific experiences were made (e.g. 'When did you first think about health? Could you please tell me about this situation?'). This method comes with a number of suggestions for how to formulate questions and for how to ask participants to recount situations (see Flick, 2014, pp. 275–8; and Flick, 2018a, Chapter 3, for examples). It can be used, for instance, for a retrospectively oriented study in

BRESCIA UNIVERSITY
COLLEGE LIBRARY

the context of situation analysis. As it includes concept-oriented questions, it can be more easily used for concept and category development in the process of data collection than the narrative interview. The situation narratives provide more context than do answers in other forms of interviews.

No matter which of the methods presented briefly here is used, we should not forget that interviewing is more than just applying a method, as Brinkmann and Kvale, underline (2018, p. 55).

Using documents

As we saw at the beginning of this chapter, documents have always been a prominent type of data in grounded theory research. Again, some practical issues will be discussed here to support the use of this kind of data.

Access and sampling

First of all, problems of selecting the right type of documents and the most appropriate documents arise. Plummer (2001, p. 17) outlines the problem of the overwhelming existence of documents in our everyday lives (such as diaries, letters, films, graffiti, websites and the like), which might be discovered and used for research purposes.

If you want to do research based on such traces of everyday processes and lives, there is an almost infinite diversity and number of documents you can use. This mass of potential research objects raises the question of which kinds and which concrete examples of documents to use in a particular study. For the selection of documents, Scott (1990) proposes four criteria, which can be useful for deciding whether or not to employ a specific document (or set of documents) for specific research: authenticity, **credibility**, representativeness and meaning (1990, p. 6). These criteria can give you an orientation on which concrete document to use or not. Beyond that you may reflect more generally about what kinds of documents you can use.

Types of documents

Rapley and Rees (2018) identify three kinds of documents to be used for research purposes: docile documents are analyzed as texts in their own right; documents collected in other forms of fieldwork support the analysis; and documents-in-action enrich ethnographic work.

Practical issues of analyzing documents as representing wider issues

Prior (2003, pp. 5–9) describes in great detail how documentary analysis may be applied to a wider range of artefacts, understood as documents of practices or activities. Beyond analyzing *texts* as documents, Prior describes how, for instance, architectural plans of mental hospitals from various periods can be analyzed as representations of concepts of madness at a specific time: for example, stricter separation of closed-up areas for mentally ill patients indicates a less tolerant concept of mental illness, whereas open wards in a hospital plan document a more integrative and open attitude to mental illness in general. When using documents in research, Coffey (2014) finally advises us 'to pay close attention to the question of *how* documents are constructed as distinctive kinds of artefacts or productions' (2014, p. 371).

ELICITED AND NATURALLY OCCURRING DATA IN GROUNDED THEORY RESEARCH

The distinction between extant and elicited documents mentioned by Charmaz in the context of using documents in grounded theory research refers to a wider discussion – whether we should use elicited or **naturally occurring data** for our studies. Potter and Shaw (2018) use this distinction for a more general discussion of social research, referring to naturalistic materials, which 'open social science up to new questions, challenging its orthodoxies, and revealing orders of social life that have fallen into the gaps between the theories and instruments of mainstream approaches' (2018). If such a position is unfolded in a consistent way, the application of methods of data collection as discussed (not only) in this chapter might become obsolete. Then we finally are driven back to Glaser's (2001) statement – 'All is data' – and his belief that we should not obstruct our analysis by using preconceived methods. Whether or not this is a practicable way for each and every study in grounded theory research or just one alternative in a wider range of methodological approaches – the natural or elicited data have to be analyzed (see Chapter 5).

DATA COLLECTION BETWEEN 'JUST DO IT' AND SYSTEMATIC APPROACHES

As this chapter should have shown, data collection is an important issue for grounded theory studies as well. However, it is sometimes downplayed in a specific form of pragmatism or reduced to a sub-problem of theoretical sampling. In other cases, it is focused on specific methods (intensive interviewing, for example) or seen as depending on which specific social world is to be studied. For some of those methods of data collection that have been part of the grounded theory research methods discourse from the beginning to current versions, some practical suggestions were made in this chapter to give you more orientation for beginning a study or starting research. This should contribute to offering a way out of the sometimes over-challenging aspiration of intuitionalism (see also Chapter 8) in grounded theory research.

KEY POINTS

- Data collection in grounded theory literature is in general a minor topic compared with sampling and analysis of materials.
- The versions of grounded theory vary in the relevance they see for systematic data collection and the use of specific methods for it.
- Ethnography, document analysis and, more recently, interviewing are the most prominent methods.
- The way such methods are described in grounded theory textbooks leaves a lot to the intuition and imagination of the individual researchers in the field.
- Some suggestions on the how-to-do level should help in giving a practical orientation on the way to good data.

FURTHER READING

Observation and ethnography

The following sources provide more details about the current state of the art in doing ethnography:

Buscatto, M. (2018) 'Doing ethnography – ways and reasons', in U. Flick (ed.), *The SAGE Handbook of Qualitative Data Collection*. London: Sage.
Coffey, A. (2018) *Doing Ethnography* (Book 3 of *The SAGE Qualitative Research Kit*, 2nd ed.). London: Sage.

Interviewing

Interviewing is spelled out in more detail in the following source:

Brinkmann, S. and Kvale, S. (2018) *Doing Interviews* (Book 2 of *The SAGE Qualitative Research Kit*, 2nd ed.). London: Sage.

Analyzing documents

The use of documents is treated in detail in the following sources:

Coffey, A. (2014) 'Analyzing documents', in U. Flick (ed.), *The SAGE Handbook of Qualitative Data Analysis*. London: Sage, pp. 367–79.

Rapley, T. (2018) *Doing Conversation, Discourse and Document Analysis* (Book 7 of *The SAGE Qualitative Research Kit*, 2nd ed.). London: Sage.

Qualitative data collection in general

Overviews of data collection in qualitative research in general can be found in the following sources:

Flick, U. (2014) *An Introduction to Qualitative Research*, 5th ed. London: Sage.

Flick, U. (ed.) (2018) *The SAGE Handbook of Qualitative Data Collection*. London: Sage.

CHAPTER FOUR

GROUNDED THEORY CODING
WAYS AND VERSIONS

CONTENTS

CHAPTER OBJECTIVES

After reading this chapter, you should understand:

- the role of coding in the various versions of grounded theory research;
- the major forms of coding in grounded theory research;
- the differences between several ways of coding in grounded theory research; and
- more about how to do coding and data analysis in the major approaches of grounded theory research.

INTRODUCTION

Now we will address the central activity in grounded theory research. Data analysis is based on coding and here we find several suggestions for how to do it. This and the next chapter aim at giving you an overview of these alternatives as an orientation regarding which of these you can use for your own study.

THE ROLE OF CODING IN GROUNDED THEORY RESEARCH

Grounded theory coding is used as a generic term to cover the different approaches that have developed over the years (Charmaz, 2014). It refers to the procedures for analyzing data that have been collected in order to develop a grounded theory. This kind of analysis was introduced by Glaser and Strauss (1967) and further elaborated by Glaser (1978), Strauss (1987), and Strauss and Corbin (1990; Corbin and Strauss, 2015), Clarke (2005) and Charmaz (2014). As already mentioned, in this approach the interpretation of data should not be regarded independently of their collection or the sampling of the material, although there are plenty of examples in which it is just used as a way of analysis. In grounded theory research, interpretation is the anchoring point for making decisions about which data or cases to integrate next in the analysis and how or with which methods they should be collected. In the years since the publication of the first introductory text by Glaser and Strauss (1967), proliferation of the approaches in the field has led to debates and distinctions about the right way to do grounded theory coding. Therefore, it makes sense to briefly outline some of the different versions of how coding proceeds, which should help you to select one of these ways of coding for your own research.

THE ORIGINAL APPROACH OF GLASER AND STRAUSS

In their original outline of the 'discovery of grounded theory', Glaser and Strauss (1967), did not describe specific forms of coding (as later versions offered). Similar to data collection (see Chapter 3), which was mainly an issue in the context of theoretical sampling, coding is largely addressed as a part of the **constant comparative method** of data analysis in a chapter that is mostly a reprint of an earlier article by Glaser (1965). Their approach to coding of qualitative data was developed in distinction to forms of coding in which qualitative data are turned into a quantifiable form or are just seen as inspirations. Their own approach is a combination of coding and theory development by constant comparison '*by using explicit coding and analytic procedures*' (Glaser and Strauss, 1967, p. 102). In this original version, for the process of developing theories, the constant comparative method as a procedure for interpreting texts is seen as more central than specific forms of coding. It basically consists of four stages: '(1) comparing incidents applicable to each category, (2) integrating categories and their properties, (3) delimiting the theory, and (4) writing the theory' (Glaser, 1969, p. 220). For Glaser, the systematic circularity of this process is an essential feature. This procedure becomes a method of *constant* comparison when analysts take care to compare coding over and over again to codes and classifications that have already been made. Material which has already been coded is not finished with after its classification: rather it is continually integrated into the further process of comparison.

In general, the first outline of the methodology provides not so much concrete advice for how to do the analysis but more a methodological distinction from other researchers' approaches (Howard Becker is often mentioned as having a different approach, or **analytic induction** in distinction from the constant comparative method, for example). However, you will find some practical orientation here as well, such as to use categories you have constructed or abstracted from the language in the field. The latter tend to label processes and behaviours and the former will tend to refer to the explanations for what you have observed (Glaser and Strauss, 1967, p. 107). However, this clarification of category development is an example of the way methodological knowledge is presented and offered. It is more a retrospective view on research that has been done or advanced to a specific step than a prospective view on how to begin, continue and proceed to undertake research. The distinctions of kinds and sources of category labels is quite helpful for reflecting the coding process but not so much an orientation for how and from where to take or develop codes or categories. More concrete advice is given in some stages and rules outlined in the text for comparison: 'Comparing incidents applicable to each category. The analyst starts by coding each incident in his data into as many categories of analysis as possible, as categories emerge or as data emerge that fit an existing category' (1967, p. 105). This stage is complemented by a 'defining rule for the constant comparative method: while coding an incident for a category, compare it with the previous incidents in the same and different groups coded in the same category' (1967, p. 106). A second rule becomes relevant at this stage and turns the analyst to writing in the process: '*stop coding and record a memo on your ideas*' (1967, p. 107) – for example, when theoretical notions resulting from coding several times for a category and clarification for how to proceed become necessary.

The second stage is to aim for 'integrating categories and their properties' (p. 108) as the coding continues, the constant comparative units change from comparison of incident with incident to comparison of incident with properties of the category that resulted from initial comparisons of incidents. For this integration of categories, properties and finally the theory, some illustrative examples are given, but mainly the integration will sort itself out if the general principles of the approach are applied. If theoretical sampling and data analysis are applied simultaneously, the integration of the 'theory is more likely to emerge by itself' (1967, p. 109).

The third stage ('*delimiting the theory*' – 1967, p. 109) refers to two levels: the theory and the categories. It includes an increasing solidification, which means less and less changes or modifications the further the coding process advances. Even more important is a continuing reduction, which allows the researcher to 'formulate the theory with a smaller set of higher level concepts. This delimits its terminology and text' (1967, p. 110). For their study *Awareness of Dying* (Glaser and Strauss, 1965a; see Case studies 1.1 and 2.1), they describe how this reduction led to a more generalized theory in the end by further reducing the terminology and transferring the substantive theory to other fields of interaction between professionals and clients, for example (Glaser and Strauss, 1967, p. 110).

At this stage, Glaser and Strauss advance beyond a mere description of processes observed in a field and analyzed by coding. They formulate their understanding of theory as an outcome of their study and which claims are linked to theory development, such as '(1) parsimony of variables and formulation, and (2) scope in the applicability of the theory to a wide range of situations ... while keeping a close correspondence of theory and data' (1967, pp. 110–11). The final stage is writing the theory (see also Chapter 7), which is to 'collate the memos on each category' (1967, p. 113).

All in all, Glaser and Strauss have outlined a process of theory development from data, which includes some major principles. (1) Data should result from theoretical sampling. (2) The analysis and collection of data should proceed in an integrated way. (3) Analysis consists of coding and constant comparison. (4) This should not only lead to a multitude of categories, but include a reduction and (5) a generalization of the theory to other areas and fields. (6) Coding should be closely linked to writing memos (7) and the memos are directly used for writing the theory. This basic understanding of coding, comparison and theory development was further developed in the 1970s by Glaser (1978), in the 1980s mainly by Strauss (1987), and in the 1990s by Strauss and Corbin (1990, 1994).

GLASER AND CLASSIC GROUNDED THEORY

In many respects, Glaser and Strauss proceed in the same way when analyzing the material. In the first of a number of textbooks about grounded theory research, Glaser (1978) spelled out the methodological procedures in grounded theory research in a more concrete way. He was then absent for a while from the methodological discussion, but more recently, Glaser (1992) has criticized the way Strauss and Corbin have elaborated their approach (see below) and in particular the coding paradigm and the idea of axial coding. In the main, he sees this as forcing a structure on the data instead of discovering what emerges as structure from the data and the analysis. He continued his critique in the new millennium with a number of textbooks and articles. His approach is also the source for a recent textbook by Holton and Walsh (2017) with the title *Classic Grounded Theory*. This book again makes the claim for defining what grounded theory research really is (as seen by the camp of Glaser and in several of his books). It mainly rewrites grounded theory research from Glaser's position and the title of the book has also recently become the label for Glaser's approach.

In his original outline, Glaser (1978) basically divides the coding process into two stages: substantive and theoretical coding. The first stage begins with open coding to generate an 'emergent set of categories and their properties which fit, work and are relevant for integrating into a theory' (1978, p. 56).

For this step, a number of rules are presented. First, to ask a set of questions: 'What is this data a study of?', 'What category or property of a category, or what part of the emerging theory does this incident indicate?' and 'What is actually happening in the data?' (1978, p. 57). The second rule refers to coding line by line and each sentence (1978, p. 57). Third, the analysts must do their own coding (1978, p. 58); and, fourth, they must always interrupt coding to memo the ideas stimulated by coding (1978, p. 58). While coding, analysts should stay within the confines of their substantive area and the field study and to be sceptical about 'any face sheet variable such as age, sex, social class, skin color etc., until it emerges as relevant' (1978, p. 60).

Glaser refers to two kinds of codes in substantive coding: *in vivo* **code**s come directly from the material, whereas *analytic codes* are in the wording of the analyst and already explain theoretically what is happening in the data. In Glaser's version, similar to Strauss's later suggestions, open coding is the first step. But then he progresses in a different way, because selective coding here is the second step and still located in the first phase (substantive coding): 'To selectively code for a core variable, then, means, that the analyst delimits his coding to only those variables that relate to the core variable in sufficiently significant way to be used in a parsimonious theory' (1978, p. 61). An important instrument here is the **concept indicator model**, 'which directs the conceptual coding of a set of empirical **indicator**s' (1978, p. 62) based on 'constant comparing of (1) indicator to indicator, and then when a conceptual code is generated (2) also comparing indicators to the emerging concept'.

The second stage in Glaser's model is *theoretical coding*. Here as a main instrument for coding material more formally and in a theoretically relevant way, Glaser (1978) has suggested a list of basic codes, which he grouped as coding families. These families are sources for defining codes and at the same time an orientation for searching new codes for a set of data (see Table 4.1). As Kelle (2007, p. 200) holds, this set of coding families comes with a lot of background assumptions not made explicit, which limits their usefulness for structuring substantive codes, in particular for beginners looking for an orientation on how to code. It can be used as an inspiration for which directions to look in if you are searching for possible links among your substantive codes.

A major aim in Glaser's version of grounded theory is to identify a core category. Glaser (1978, pp. 94–5) has developed a number of criteria for what qualifies a code or category as a core category. It (1) must be central, (2) reoccur frequently, (3) therefore takes more time to saturate. (4) The connections with other categories come quick and richly and (5) it should have clear and 'grabbing' implications for formal theory and (6) a considerable carry through, which means it does not lead to dead ends. (7) It is completely variable in degree, dimension and type. (8) It is also a dimension of the problem and (9) tends to prevent two other sources (social interest and logical deductive) from establishing a core which is not grounded. (10) It can be any kind of theoretical code: a process, a condition, dimensions, a consequence. This notion raises the question of the status of a core category – is it the main result of the research process or is it a means for understanding the issue of the study?

TABLE 4.1 Coding families applied to examples of coding pain experiences

Coding families	Concepts	Examples
The six Cs	Causes, contexts, contingencies, consequences, covariances, conditions	Causes of pain Conditions of suffering from pain
Process	Stages, phases, phasings, transitions, passages, careers, chains, sequences	Career of a patient with chronic pain
Basic family	Basic social process, basic social psychological process, basic social structural condition, etc.	Ignorance of pain Coping with pain
Cultural family	Social norms, social values, social beliefs	Social norms about tolerating pain, 'feeling rules'
Strategy family	Strategies, tactics, techniques, mechanisms, management	Strategies of coping with pain Techniques for reducing pain
Degree family	Extent, level, intensity, range, amount, continuum, statistical average, standard deviation	Extent of pain suffering
Type family	Types, classes, genres, prototypes, styles, kinds	Types of pain, e.g. burning, piercing, throbbing, shooting, stinging, gnawing, sharp
Interactive family	Interaction, mutual effects, interdependence, reciprocity, asymmetries, rituals	Interaction of pain experience and coping Rituals of communicating about pain
Dimension family	Dimensions, sector, segment, part, aspect, section, etc.	Modest–strong pain Punctual–permanent pain
Identity/self family	Identity, self-image, self-concept, self-evaluation, social worth, transformations of self	Self-concepts of pain in patients Shifts in identity after continuous pain experience
Cutting point family	Boundary, critical juncture, cutting point, turning point, tolerance levels, point of no return	Turning point: when did the pain become chronic? New level in the medical career of pain patient
Consensus family	Contracts, agreements, definitions of the situation, uniformity, conformity, conflict	Compliance of the patient: taking pills according to the prescription
Paired opposite family	Ingroup–outgroup, in–out, manifest–latent, explicit–implicit, overt–covert, informal–formal, etc.	Patients with pain – pain free peers Overt communication of pain – attempts to hide pain
Cutting point family	Boundary, cutting point, turning point, breaking point, deviance, etc.	Point when pain becomes unbearable Point when pain became permanent

Sources: Adapted and modified from Glaser (1978, pp. 75–82) and Thornberg and Charmaz (2014, p. 160)

CODING IN THE STRAUSS AND CORBIN APPROACH

Strauss's introduction

Strauss (1987) has outlined his own version of the process of interpretation in grounded theory research and provided some more details on the how-to-do level.

He did not take up some of the essentials of Glaser's (1978) approach – for example, neither the part of the coding process Glaser calls 'theoretical coding' (see above), nor the idea of 'coding families'. A central aspect is the concept of the 'coding paradigm' and the new step of axial coding, which it is part of. Open coding in Strauss's book means to start by 'scrutinizing the field note, interview, or other document very closely; line by line or even word by word. The aim is to produce concepts that seem to fit the data' (Strauss, 1987, p. 28). The coding paradigm aims at elaborating the relations between categories and to develop structures in the data. The coding paradigm 'is central to the coding procedures ... it functions as a reminder to code data for relevance to whatever phenomena are referenced by a given category for the following: conditions, interactions among the actors, strategies and tactics, consequences (Strauss, 1987, p. 27–8).

Strauss picks up a lot of suggestions made by Glaser for open and selective coding (see above), but unlike Glaser locates selective coding more toward the end of theory development. His new step, axial coding, is 'an essential aspect of the open coding. It consists of intense analysis done around one category at a time, in terms of the paradigm items' (1987, p. 32). It leads to understanding relations between several categories and of categories to subcategories. Strauss maintains the distinction between *in vivo* codes from the material and – in his terms – sociologically constructed codes (1987, p. 33).

Strauss and Corbin's further elaboration

Strauss and Corbin (1990) further developed this approach to describing the methods and provide, as they characterize it, a number of 'procedures' for working with text that can be differentiated. They maintain the concepts of 'open coding,' and 'selective coding' similar to Glaser, although the latter is the third and final step here as well. They also apply axial coding as a second form of coding which follows open coding. These three procedures are neither seen as clearly distinguishable procedures nor as temporally separated phases in the process. Rather, they are different ways of handling textual material between which you move back and forth if necessary and which you combine. But the process of interpretation begins with open coding, whereas towards the end of the whole analytical process, selective coding comes more to the fore. Coding here is understood as representing the operations by which data are broken down, conceptualized, and put back together in new ways. It is the central process by which theories are built from data (Strauss and Corbin, 1990, p. 3).

According to this understanding, coding includes the constant comparison of phenomena, cases, concepts, and so on, and the formulation of questions that are addressed to the text. Starting from the data, the process of coding leads to the development of theories through a process of abstraction. Concepts or codes are attached to the empirical material. They are first formulated as closely as possible to the text, and later more and more abstractly. **Categorizing** in this procedure refers to the summary of such concepts into *generic concepts* and to the elaboration of the relations between concepts and generic concepts or categories and superior concepts. The development of theory involves the formulation of *networks* of categories or concepts and the relations between them. Relations may be elaborated between superior and inferior categories (hierarchically) but also between concepts at the same level. During the whole process, impressions, associations, questions, ideas, and so on are noted in *memos*, which complement and explain the codes that were found (see Chapter 7).

Open coding

This first step aims at expressing data and phenomena in the form of concepts. For this purpose, data are first disentangled ('segmented'). Units of meaning classify expressions (single words, short sequences of words) in order to attach annotations and 'concepts' (codes) to them. Box 4.1 includes an example from my own studies, in which a subjective definition of health and the first codes attached to this piece of text are presented. This example should clarify the procedure. A slash separates two sections in the interview passage from each other and each superscript number indicates a section. The notes for each section are then presented: in some cases these led to the formulation of codes and in other cases they were abandoned in the further proceedings as being less suitable.

BOX 4.1 EXAMPLE OF SEGMENTATION AND OPEN CODING

This example comes from one of my projects about health concepts of lay people. It demonstrates how one of the analysts applied the **segmentation** of a passage in one of the interviews in the context of open coding in order to develop codes. In this process, the analyst explored a number of associations more or less helpful or close to the original passage:

Well-I[1]/link[2]/personally[3]/to health[4]/: the complete functionality[5]/of the human organism[6]/all[7]/the biochemical processes[8] of the organism[9]/included in this[10]/all cycles[11]/but also[12]/the mental state[13]/of my person[14]/and of Man in general[15]/.

(Continued)

(Continued)

First associations on the way to codes

1. Starting shot, introduction.
2. Making connections.
3. Interviewee emphasizes the reference to himself, delimiting from others, local commonplace. He does not need to search first.
4. See 2, taking up the question.
5. Technical, learned, textbook expression, model of the machine, norm orientation, thinking in norms, normative claim (someone who does not fully function is ill).

Codes: functionality, normative claim

6. Distancing, general, contradiction to the introduction (announcement of a personal idea), textbook, reference to Man, but as a machine.

Code: mechanistic image of Man

7. Associations to 'all": referring to a complete, comprehensive, maximal understanding of health .... however, 'all' does not include much differentiation.
8. Prison, closed system, there is something outside, passive, other directed, possibly an own dynamic of the included.
9. See 6.
10. Textbook category.
11. Comprehensive; model of the machine, circle of rules, procedure according to rules, opposite to chaos.

Code: mechanistic–somatic idea of health

12. Complement, new aspect opposite to what was said before, two (or more) different things belonging to the concept of health.

Code: multidimensionality

13. Static ('what is his state?'); mechanistic concept of human being ('state') ...
14. Mentions something personal, produces a distance again immediately, talks very neutrally about what concerns him, defence against too much proximity to the female interviewer and to himself.

Code: wavering between personal and general level

15. General, abstract image of Man, norm orientedness, singularity easier to over-look.

Code: distance

This procedure is not meant to be applied to the whole text of an interview or an observation protocol. Rather, it is used for particularly instructive or perhaps extremely unclear passages. Often the beginning of a text is the starting point. This procedure serves to elaborate a deeper understanding of the text. Sometimes dozens of codes result from open coding. The next step in the procedure is to categorize these codes by grouping them around phenomena discovered in the data, which are particularly relevant to the research question. The resulting categories are again linked to codes, which are now more abstract than those used in the first step. Codes now should represent the content of a category in a striking way and above all should offer an aid to remembering the reference of the category. Possible sources for labelling codes are concepts borrowed from the social science literature (*constructed* codes) or taken from interviewees' expressions (*in vivo* codes). Of the two types of code, the latter are preferred because they are closer to the studied material. The categories found in this way are then further developed. To this end the properties belonging to a category are labelled and dimensionalized (i.e. located along a continuum in order to define the category more precisely regarding its content). To explain more precisely what they mean by properties and dimensions, Strauss and Corbin use the concept of 'colour' as an example. Its properties include 'shade, intensity, hue, and so on. Each of these properties can be dimensionalized. Thus, color can vary in shade from dark to light, in intensity from high to low, and in hue from bright to dull. Shade, intensity, and hue are what might be called general properties' (1990, p. 70).

Open coding may be applied in various degrees of detail. A text can be coded line by line, sentence by sentence, or paragraph by paragraph, or a code can be linked to whole texts (a protocol, a case, etc.). Which of these alternatives you should apply will depend on your research question, on your material, on your personal style as analyst, and on the stage that your research has reached. It is important not to lose touch with the aims of coding. The main goal is to break down and understand a text and to attach and develop categories and put them into an order in the course of time. Open coding aims at developing substantial codes describing, naming, or classifying the phenomenon under study or a certain aspect of it. Strauss and Corbin summarize open coding as follows:

Concepts are the basic building blocks of theory. Open coding in grounded theory method is the analytic process by which concepts are identified and developed in terms of their properties and dimensions. The basic analytic procedures by which this is accomplished are: the asking of questions about the data; and the making of comparisons for similarities and differences between each incident, event and other instances of phenomena. Similar events and incidents are labelled and grouped to form categories. (1990, p. 74)

The result of open coding should be a list of the codes and categories attached to the text. This should be complemented by the code notes that were produced to explain and define the content of codes and categories, and a multitude of memos, which contain striking observations on the material and thoughts that are relevant to the development of the theory.

For both open coding and the other coding strategies it is suggested that the researchers regularly address the text with the following list of so-called basic questions, such as: What (is the issue)? Who (is involved)? How (aspects of the phenomenon), when, how long, where (does something occur)? How much, why (reasons), by which means and strategies shall goals be reached?

By asking these questions, the text will be opened up. You may address them to single passages, but also to whole cases. In addition to these questions, comparisons between the extremes of a dimension ('flip-flop technique': Strauss and Corbin, 1990, p. 84) or to phenomena from completely different contexts and a consequent questioning of self-evidence ('waving-the-red-flag technique', p. 91) are possible ways to further untangle the dimensions and contents of a category.

Axial coding

After identifying a number of substantive categories, the next step is to refine and differentiate the categories resulting from open coding. As a second step, Strauss and Corbin suggest doing more formal coding to identify and classify links between substantive categories. In axial coding, the relations between categories are elaborated. In order to formulate such relations, Strauss and Corbin (1990, p. 124) suggest selective coding again using the coding paradigm model, which is shown in Figure 4.1.

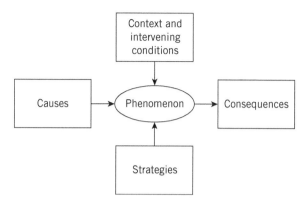

FIGURE 4.1 The coding paradigm model

This very simple and, at the same time, very general model serves to clarify the relations between a phenomenon, its causes and consequences, its context, and the strategies of those who are involved. This model is based on two axes: one goes from causes to phenomena and to consequences, the other one links context, intervening conditions, and actions and interactional strategies of participants to the phenomenon.

Concepts may be classified in four ways: (1) as *phenomena* for this category; (2) as *context* or *conditions* for other categories; (3) as *consequences*; and finally (4) as *strategies*. It is important to note that the coding paradigm only names possible relations between phenomena and concepts: the purpose of coding is to facilitate the discovery or establishment of structures of relations between phenomena, between concepts, and between categories. Here as well, the questions addressed to the text and the comparative strategies mentioned above are employed once again in a complementary way.

The developed relations and the categories that are treated as essential are repeatedly verified against the text and the data. The researcher moves continuously back and forth between inductive thinking (developing concepts, categories and relations from the text) and deductive thinking (testing the concepts, categories and relations against the text, especially against passages or cases that are different from those from which they were developed). Axial coding is summarized as a 'complex process of inductive and deductive thinking involving several steps … toward discovering and relating categories in terms of the paradigm model' (Strauss and Corbin, 1990, p. 114).

In axial coding, the categories that are most relevant to the research question are selected from the developed codes and the related code notes. Many different passages in the text are then sought as evidence of these relevant codes in order to elaborate the axial category on the basis of the questions mentioned above. In order to structure the intermediate results (means–end, cause–effect, temporal, or local) relations are elaborated between the different axial categories by using the parts of the coding paradigm mentioned above.

From the multitude of categories that were originated, those which seem to be most promising for further elaboration are selected. These axial categories are enriched by their fit with as many passages as possible. For further refining, the questions and comparisons mentioned above are employed.

Selective coding

The third step, selective coding, continues the axial coding at a higher level of abstraction. This step elaborates the development and integration of axial coding in comparison with other groups and focuses on potential core concepts or core variables. In this step you will look for further examples and evidence for relevant categories. This then leads to an elaboration or formulation of the *story of the case*. At this point, Strauss and Corbin conceive the issue or the central phenomenon of the study as a case and not a person or a single interview. One should bear in mind here that the aim of this formulation is to give a short descriptive overview of the story and the case and it should therefore comprise only a few sentences. The analysis goes beyond this descriptive level when the *story line* is elaborated – a concept is attached to the central phenomenon of the story and related to the other categories. In any case, the result should be *one* central category and *one* central phenomenon. The analyst must decide between equally salient phenomena and weigh them, so that one central category results, together with the subcategories which are related to it. The core category again is developed in its features and dimensions and linked to (all, if possible) other categories by using the parts and relations of the coding paradigm. The analysis and the development of the theory aim at discovering patterns in the data as well as the conditions under which these apply. Grouping the data according to the coding paradigm gives specificity to the theory and enables the researcher to say, 'Under these conditions (listing them) this happens; whereas under these conditions, this is what occurs' (Strauss and Corbin, 1990, pp. 130–1).

Finally, the theory is formulated in greater detail and again checked against the data. The procedure of interpreting data, like the integration of additional material, ends at the point where theoretical saturation has been reached (i.e. further coding, enrichment of categories, and so on no longer provide or promise new knowledge). At the same time, the procedure is flexible enough that the researcher can re-enter the same source texts and the same codes from open coding with a different research question and aim at developing and formulating a grounded theory of a different issue (See Case study 4.1).

CASE STUDY 4.1   UNENDING WORK AND CARE

Juliet Corbin and Anselm Strauss further developed and applied the approach of grounded theory coding in many studies in the context of nursing and medical sociology in the 1980s and since. In one of their studies, Corbin and Strauss (1988) applied their methodology to the study of how people experiencing a chronic illness and their relatives manage to deal with this serious illness and manage to conduct their personal lives.

The empirical basis of this study was a number of intensive interviews with such couples at home and at work. These were undertaken to identify the problems these couples faced in their personal lives in order to answer the question: 'How can the chronically ill be helped to manage their illnesses more effectively?' (Corbin and Strauss, 1988, p. xi).

Different from early conceptualizations of grounded theory research in which it was suggested *not* to develop a theoretical framework and understanding of the issue under study (e.g. in Glaser and Strauss, 1967), the authors here start with an extensive presentation of the theoretical tools used in their study, which builds on previous empirical work by the same researchers.

The main concept in the research is 'trajectory'. This refers to the course of the illness as well as to the work of the people who attempt to control and shape this course. Corbin and Strauss identify several stages – trajectory phases – that are labelled as acute, comeback, stable, unstable, deteriorating and dying stages of illness. In the theoretical framework, the authors analyze how a chronically ill member of a family changes the life plans of families, and focus on biographical processes with which the victims try to manage and come to terms with the illness. In the second part of their book, Corbin and Strauss use this theoretical framework to analyze the various trajectory phases in greater detail.

This is not only one of the most important studies in the field of everyday management of chronic illness. It is also very fruitful in developing and differentiating a theoretical framework for this issue, which goes beyond existing concepts of coping, adjustment and stress. The authors develop from their empirical work a much more elaborate concept (trajectory) for analyzing the experience of their research partners. They achieve this by analyzing the different trajectory stages by asking a set of questions: 'What are the different types of work? How do they get done? How do the central work processes and interactional developments enter into getting the work done? What are the biographical processes that accompany and affect those matters?' (1988, p. 168). All in all, this study is a very good example of how the research strategy developed by Glaser, Strauss and Corbin can be used for analyzing a theoretically and practically relevant issue in several steps.

Strauss and Corbin complemented their coding strategies by introducing the **conditional matrix** as another tool for grounded theory research, for mapping conditions and consequences at several levels. In the original version (see 1990, p. 163), which has been differentiated and detailed in later editions of their book, 'action pertaining to a phenomenon' is seen as embedded in widening circles of contexts reaching from interaction, to group/individual/collective, sub-organizational/ sub-institutional level, organizational and institutional level, community, national, international.

In the years since 1990 and in particular after Strauss's death in 1996, there have been several updates of the book, now with the authorship given as Corbin and Strauss (e.g. 2015), in which the orientation has not really shifted, whereas the procedures have not really gained clarity in the way they are presented (see Chapter 5).

In this chapter the focus has been on the main versions of coding in grounded theory, which made the approach prominent and successful in the development of qualitative research from the 1960s until the 1990s. One outcome of these developments and the success of the approach was the battle about the 'right' way of doing grounded theory research and who, Strauss or Glaser, should have the definitional power to delineate what is right and wrong and what is grounded theory. In the following chapter, we will turn to the more recent attempts to settle the approach, end the battles and connect it to more recent discourses in qualitative research.

● KEY POINTS

- Glaser and Strauss's original version (1967) gives a good orientation about the programme of grounded theory research and data analysis in it. It is more to do with spelling out the attitude of grounded theory research and less with concrete suggestions on the how-to-do level.
- Glaser (1978) provides a more practical orientation in spelling out the approach.
- Strauss (1987) also makes how to proceed in the analysis of qualitative data more transparent.
- Strauss and Corbin (1990, and onward) turn the approach much more to concrete recipes, instruments and procedures.
- These approaches can be seen as mutually exclusive ways of doing grounded theory research, or as suggestions for how to do it that can be combined on a more practical level.

■ FURTHER READING

Still the classic text:

Glaser, B.G. and Strauss, A.L. (1967) *The Discovery of Grounded Theory: Strategies for Qualitative Research*. Chicago: Aldine.

For more on variations of the method:

Glaser, B.G. (1978) *Theoretical Sensitivity: Advances in the Methodology of Grounded Theory*. Mill Valley, CA: Sociology Press.

Strauss, A.L. (1987) *Qualitative Analysis for Social Scientists*. New York: Cambridge University Press.

Strauss, A.L. and Corbin, J. (1990) *Basics of Qualitative Research: Grounded Theory Procedures and Techniques*. Newbury Park, CA: Sage.

For more on qualitative data analysis in general and by using **CAQDAS software**:

Gibbs, G.R. (2018) *Analyzing Qualitative Data* (Book 6 of *The SAGE Qualitative Research Kit*, 2nd ed.). London: Sage.

CHAPTER FIVE

GOING AHEAD

RECENT DEVELOPMENTS IN GROUNDED THEORY DATA ANALYSIS

CONTENTS

CHAPTER OBJECTIVES

After reading this chapter, you should know:

- how constructivist grounded theory integrates the various versions of grounded theory research;
- the major forms of coding in this approach in grounded theory research;
- how classic grounded theory developed further;
- suggestions and approaches for data analysis in situational analysis;
- more about how to use coding in analyzing interviews and cases; and
- about which approach to choose or which parts of approaches to combine in coding our data.

AFTER THE BATTLES

The years from the 1970s until the early 1990s were characterized by an advancing elaboration and diversification of grounded theory analysis by the 'fathers' Glaser and Strauss. In the 1990s a battle between them began about what grounded theory is and is not. This manifested mainly in a series of books by Barney Glaser who re-entered the arena in the 1990s reacting against the publication and success of Strauss's book (1987) and in particular of Strauss and Corbin's textbook (1990). Strauss had selectively included but also excluded several of Glaser's ideas. There was a battle about definitional power between the two schools inside grounded theory research. However, there were also some attacks on grounded theory as an approach from outside. This had to do with fear of domination by this approach when computer-assisted qualitative data analysis (CAQDAS) began to be used in the late 1990s and was basically oriented around grounded theory as the way qualitative research was done. For example, **ATLAS.ti** was developed using the Strauss and Corbin (1990) book as a model for what to implement.

Other attacks on grounded theory came from outside the area in the context of more interpretative research or of postmodernism (see Atkinson et al., 2003) or of **constructivism**. This was often a debate about epistemologies (see Chapter 1) but became concrete in the way the analysis was done and mainly addressed the idea of coding. In this situation of internal and external debates and attacks, a number of approaches were developed by second-generation grounded theorists (see the contributions to Morse et al., 2009) to resettle grounded theory as a contemporary way of doing research rather than a battlefield. In this chapter some of these newer approaches are discussed and complemented by some additional suggestions for closing some gaps in grounded theory research. The first two approaches further develop the idea of coding, in the tradition of the founding fathers. The third approach goes in a different direction and the fourth returns to coding but from a different angle.

CONSTRUCTIVIST GROUNDED THEORY

Since around 2000, Kathy Charmaz's constructivist reformulation of the whole approach (e.g. Charmaz, 2014; Thornberg and Charmaz, 2014; Bryant and Charmaz, 2007b) has become the most prominent version of grounded theory research. Charmaz has also updated the concept and vocabulary of data analysis in grounded theory. She sticks to coding as the main analytic activity and maintains many of the ideas of the two founding fathers. Her whole approach can be read as an effort to make grounded theory analysis more manageable and easier to do. Similar to Clarke with situational analysis (2005, see below), Charmaz also works to save grounded theory as an approach from becoming outdated by engaging in discussions in broader contexts of qualitative research discussions and publications (e.g. in handbook chapters) to establish grounded theory in the wider field of qualitative research. But at the same time constructivist grounded theory can be read as an attempt to bridge the gaps that have developed between the Strauss and Glaser lines of discussion and to re-establish grounded theory as one school of qualitative research instead of a battlefield for opponents fighting over the right way of doing this kind of research. The main arena in which the battles about the right way of doing grounded theory research have been fought, and thus the one where peace had to be established, is the conceptualization of data analysis and mainly of coding. For Charmaz, coding means to label segments of data. Labels should summarize and account for the segments they refer to (2014, p. 111). Charmaz suggests doing open coding line by line, because it 'also helps you to refrain from imputing your motives, fears, or unresolved personal issues to your respondents and to your collected data' (2003, p. 94). Coding in general is suggested here to be done with gerunds (noun forms of verbs) as this helps the researchers to detect and remain focused on process and action (Charmaz, 2014). Her approach includes three ways of coding: initial, focused and theoretical coding.

Initial coding

Thornberg and Charmaz (2014, p. 156) outline initial coding (their equivalent to open coding) as comparing data to data. Researchers should explore and interpret what is going on in the data and produce 'short, simple, precise and active' codes. In this conception, the development of codes is the central aim and researchers should remain open to what is happening in the data. The constant comparative method is applied and should direct the coding as an attitude. They also take in Glaser's suggestions for questions to ask of the data as an orientation, but extend them by some more focused questions such as: 'What process(es) is at issue here? How can I define it?' 'How does this process develop?' 'How does the research participant(s) act and profess to think and feel while involved in this process?' (Thornberg and Charmaz, 2014, p. 156).

Charmaz gives a concrete example of this procedure, shown in Box 5.1. The codes Charmaz developed can be found in the left column and an excerpt from the interview is in the right column of the box.

BOX 5.1 EXAMPLE OF INITIAL LINE BY LINE CODING

Shifting symptoms, having inconsistent days	If you have lupus, I mean one day it's my liver; one day it's my joints; one day it's my head, and
Interpreting images of self given by others	it's like people really think you're a hypochondriac if you keep complaining about
Avoiding disclosure	different ailments ... It's like you don't want to say anything because people are going to start
Predicting rejection	thinking, you know, 'God, don't go near her, all she is – is complaining about this.' And I think
Keeping others unaware	that's why I never say anything because I feel
Seeing symptoms as connected	like everything I have is related one way or
Having others unaware	another to the lupus but most of the people don't
Anticipating disbelief	know I have lupus, and even those that do are not
Controlling others' views	going to believe that ten ailments are the
Avoiding stigma	same thing. And I don't want anybody saying,
Assessing potential losses and risks of disclosing	you know, [that] they don't want to come around me because I complain.

(Charmaz, 2003, p. 96)

Focused coding

The second step in Charmaz's approach to working with data is called focused coding, when the researchers 'will eventually "discover" the most significant or frequent initial codes that make the most analytical sense. In focused coding (also known as *selective coding*), the researcher uses these codes ... to sift through large amounts of data' (Thornberg and Charmaz, 2014, p. 158). After line by line coding at the beginning (see Box 5.1), she continues by exploring some of the resulting codes more deeply. In the example given in Box 5.1, these were the two codes 'avoiding disclosure' and 'assessing potential losses and risks of disclosing' (highlighted in bold). In this step, codes are assessed for their relevance and for becoming conceptual categories in the continuing process or analysis, and relationships between them are assessed.

Abduction as a principle in focused coding

Induction alone is not sufficient for describing inferences in the grounded theory research process. Deduction does not cover what is intended in this process. Both these factors made the discovery of abduction and abductive reasoning hot topics in the methodological discussion around constructivist grounded theory. They are relevant for coding as the core of the research process here, although most reflections about them refer either to philosophies of grounded theory research (see Chapter 1; and Bryant, 2017), to theoretical sampling (see Chapter 6; and Charmaz, 2014), or to the whole process of grounded theory with implications for data analysis: 'Grounded theory starts with an inductive logic but moves into abductive reasoning as the researcher seeks to understand emergent empirical findings. Abductive reasoning aims to account for surprises, anomalies, or puzzles in the collected data' (Charmaz, 2008, p. 157). Here imaginative interpretations of all possible accounts for the data are used for checking hypotheses and finding the most plausible interpretations. The main aspect in coding and analysis of data is that abductive thinking becomes relevant for understanding and classifying surprising findings in the data. It emphasizes the role of the researchers in the process of analysis and what they see, discover, and set up as links and possible extensions of their theory. Here the close link between imagination, fantasy and creativity in coding and abduction as an inference principle becomes visible – not to forget intuition: 'Abductive reasoning can take the researcher into unanticipated theoretical realms' (2008, p. 157).

Theoretical coding

The third step suggested by Charmaz is based on Glaser's concept of theoretical coding but advances it in one essential aspect. Charmaz explicitly refers to using concepts from the literature and existing theories as well as different types of analytic logic from pre-existing theories. Charmaz and her co-authors retain many of the suggestions made by Strauss (with or without Corbin) *and* Glaser (and followers) within the current understanding of grounded theory coding. For example, Charmaz also sees a place for axial coding (2014, p. 147) even after Corbin stopped emphasizing it as a step from the third edition of her book with Strauss (Corbin and Strauss, 2008, 2015 onward). Charmaz's concept of initial coding is a clarification of open coding in the senses of Strauss and Glaser. She suggests focused coding as a major and second step, but according to Thornberg and Charmaz (2014, p. 158) this is very similar to selective coding in the sense of Glaser. Her version of theoretical coding, as the last step, is less driven by Glaser's earlier demand to stay away from using existing concepts and theories for one's own analysis, but sees their use more openly. In Case study 5.1, an example of using this approach is outlined.

CASE STUDY 5.1 CONSTRUCTIVIST GROUNDED THEORY: IDENTITY DILEMMAS OF CHRONICALLY ILL MEN

Kathy Charmaz (1997) did a grounded theory study interested in gender and identity in the context of chronic illness. Research questions were for example: What is it like to be an active productive man one moment and a patient who faces death the next? What is it like to change one's view of oneself accordingly? Which identity dilemma does living with continued uncertainty pose for men? How do they handle this? When do they make identity changes? When do they try to preserve a former self? (1997, p. 38). Her research was based on 40 interviews with 20 men with chronic illness; 80 interviews with chronically ill women were used for comparative purposes. Her sampling focused on (1) adult status (more than 21 years of age), (2) a diagnosis of a serious, but not terminal chronic illness, (3) a disease with an uncertain course, and (4) effects of illness upon daily life (1997, p. 39) The steps in her research included: analysis of the interviews for gender differences, a thematic analysis of the men's interviews, building analytic categories from men's definitions of their situations, further interviews to refine these categories, rereading the data with a gender perspective, studying a new set of personal accounts and making comparisons with women on selected key points. She answered her research questions by looking at four major processes in men's experience of chronic illness: (1) awakening to death after a life-threatening crisis, (2) accommodating to uncertainty once the lasting consequences of the illness were recognized by the men, (3) defining illness and disability, and (4) preserving a self to maintain a sense of coherence while experiencing loss and change (1997, p. 38). This again is discussed from a comparative focus on how participants were 'preserving a public identity' and 'changing a private identity' and finally of 'strategies for preserving self'. A core element of her grounded theory was how men maintain an identity and/or sink into depression facing their permanent illness and disability: 'Life becomes struggling to live while waiting to die' (1997, p. 57).

This research was done by one of the major protagonists of grounded theory methodology. It uses core elements of the methodology, although it is neither entirely clear how far the sampling is based on theoretical sampling, nor exactly which of the coding strategies were used to analyze the data. The study provides interesting and important insights about living with chronic illness and fills relevant blanks in the theoretical knowledge about this issue. However, what becomes visible as a grounded theory is less clearly shaped than what Glaser and Strauss (1965a), for example, presented as their theory of 'awareness of dying'. This research therefore is an example of how differently grounded theory research can be pursued, without leaving the framework of the approach.

All in all, constructivist grounded theory has reformulated and updated the understanding of grounded theory coding with its emphasis on abduction and by trying to re-integrate the Straussian approach and the Glaserian critiques and ways of doing grounded theory. However, the critique coming from Glaser and his followers has also turned against constructivist grounded theory and led to a continuous second string of doing grounded theory being presented.

CLASSIC GROUNDED THEORY

Judith Holton has been active as a co-author for some of the articles in which Glaser (e.g. Glaser with Holton, 2004) reclaimed the definitional authority about what grounded theory is, first against Strauss, and then against Strauss and Corbin and Charmaz. Holton and Walsh (2017) have further elaborated Glaser's classic grounded theory. In this context, they have shifted the focus of the analysis: to 'discovery of a latent pattern of social behaviour that explains a main issue or concern within an area of research interest' (2017, p. 76). This pattern is seen as the core category and expected to emerge in open coding of data. The main way to theoretical coding emerges 'through intensive handsorting of analytic memos' (2017, p. 77). The shift is manifested by the focus on latent patterns, which go beyond what participants are aware of or beyond specific incidents. The discovery of latent patterns is a strongly interpretative act by the researchers and involves them much more than the original idea of emergence. Holton and Walsh use Glaser's distinction between substantive and theoretical coding and emphasize that theoretical coding begins 'only after all substantive coding is completed and the core category and related concepts have been theoretically saturated' (2017, p. 105). They also maintain the idea of a core category but add the idea that it refers to a latent pattern. In their update of classic grounded theory they abandon the idea of coding families but stress theoretical sorting which should be done by hand. They also take up the distinction of the types of coding suggested by Glaser and the idea of constant comparison. In addition, they stick to the idea that a code or category has to earn its relevance and should not be seen as relevant beforehand. Glaser had underlined this principle for demographic categories but they extend it to any kind of category.

CASE-ORIENTED THEMATIC CODING

When interviews are used, the link to the single case (i.e. the interviewee) is often difficult to maintain in grounded theory analysis. An alternative way of doing the analysis is briefly outlined next. This procedure was developed in the 1990s in the context of a study on technological change in everyday life in various contexts (Flick, 1996). This was set against the background of limitations in grounded theory coding (e.g. Strauss, 1987), which became evident in analyzing the data in this project. The aim was to use grounded theory coding for comparative studies in which the groups under study were derived from the research question and thus defined *a priori*. The issue of the research was the social distribution of perspectives on a phenomenon or a process. The underlying assumption was that in different social worlds or groups, differing views can be found. To assess this assumption and to identify patterns in such groups' specific ways of seeing and experiencing, it proved necessary to modify some details of the grounded theory procedures in order to increase the comparability of the empirical material. Sampling was oriented to the groups whose perspectives on the issue seemed to be most instructive for analysis, and which, therefore, were defined in advance and not derived from the state of interpretation (in contrast to more integrative grounded theory procedures). Theoretical sampling, however, then was applied in each group in order to select the concrete cases of interviewees to be studied according to the state of the analysis and category development. Correspondingly, the collection of data was conducted with a method designed to guarantee comparability by defining topics whilst at the same time remaining open to the views related to them. This may be achieved through, for example, episodic interviewing (see Chapters 3 and 9; and Flick, 2018a) in which the topic domains defined, concerning the situations to be recounted, are linked either to the issue of the study or to other forms of interviews.

The procedure of thematic coding

In the interpretation of the material, **thematic coding** is applied as a multi-stage procedure – again, with respect to the comparability of the analyses. The first step addresses the cases involved, which will be interpreted in a series of case studies.

Short description of each case

The first step is to produce a short description of each case, i.e. each participant, which is continuously checked – and modified if necessary – during the further interpretation of the case. Such a case description includes several elements. The first is a statement which is typical for the interview(ee) – the 'motto' of the case. A short description should provide information about the person with regard to the research question (e.g. age, profession, number of children, if these are relevant for the issue under study). Finally, the central topics mentioned by the interviewee concerning the research issue are summarized. After finishing the case analysis, this case description comes to form part of the results. The example in Box 5.2 is from our comparative study on everyday knowledge about technological change in different professional groups (Flick, 1996) mentioned above.

BOX 5.2   SHORT DESCRIPTION OF A CASE

For me, technology has a reassuring side

The interviewee is a female French information technology engineer, 43 years old and with a son aged 15. She has been working for about 20 years in various research institutes. At present, she works in a large institute of social science research in the computer centre and is responsible for developing software, teaching and advising employees. Technology has a lot to do with security and clarity for her. To mistrust technology would produce problems for her professional self-awareness. To master technology is important for her self-concept. She narrates a good deal, using juxtapositions of leisure, nature, feeling and family against technology and work, and she repeatedly mentions the cultural benefit from technologies, especially from television.

Developing a thematic structure

In contrast to the grounded theory procedures outlined above, first a deepening analysis of a single case (i.e. the first interview) will be carried out. This case analysis pursues several aims: one is to preserve and elucidate the relations between meanings that the interviewee presents concerning the topic of the study. This is why a case study is done for all cases in the study.

A second aim is to develop a system of categories for the analysis of the single case. To elaborate this system of categories (similar to grounded theory), it is necessary to apply, first, open coding and then selective coding. Here, selective coding aims less at developing a grounded core category across all cases than at generating thematic domains and categories for the single case first.

After analyzing the first cases, the categories and thematic domains identified for each case should be cross-checked. From this cross-checking a thematic structure results: this will then underlie the analysis of further cases in order to increase their comparability. The excerpts given in Box 5.3 as an example (of such a thematic structure), come from our study on technological change in everyday life previously mentioned (Flick, 1996).

BOX 5.3 EXAMPLE OF THEMATIC STRUCTURE OF CASE ANALYSIS

1. First encounter with technology
2. Definition of technology
3. Computers
   3.1 Definition
   3.2 First encounter(s) with computers
   3.3 Professional handling of computers
   3.4 Changes in communication due to computers
4. Television
   4.1 Definition
   4.2 First encounter(s) with television
   4.3 Present meaning
5. Alterations due to technological change
   5.1 Everyday life
   5.2 Household equipment

The structure in Box 5.3 was developed from the first cases and then continually assessed for all further cases. It will need to be modified if new or contradictory aspects emerge. It is used to analyze all cases that are part of the interpretation.

Fine interpretation of thematic domains: key questions

For a fine interpretation of the thematic domains, single passages of the text (e.g. narratives of situations) are analyzed in detail. The coding paradigm suggested by Strauss (1987, pp. 27–8) was taken as a starting point for developing the following key questions:

1. *Conditions:* Why? What has led to the situation? Background? Course?
2. *Interaction among the actors:* Who acted? What happened?
3. *Strategies and tactics:* Which ways of handling situations were used, e.g. avoidance, adaptation?
4. *Consequences:* What changed? Consequences? Results?

The result of this process is a case-oriented display of the way the case specifically deals with the issue of the study. This result includes constantly recurring topics (e.g. strangeness of technology) that can be found in the viewpoints across different domains (e.g. work, leisure, household).

In the further progress of the analysis, selective coding of material to the parts of the thematic structure is applied. The thematic structure thus developed may also serve for comparing cases and groups (i.e. for elaborating correspondences and differences between the various groups in the study). Thus the social distribution of perspectives on the issue under study are analyzed and assessed. For example, after the case analyses have shown that the subjective definition of technology is an essential thematic domain for understanding technological change, it is then possible to compare the definitions of technology and the related coding from all cases. In the further development of this case-based analysis, more detailed case studies of single interviewees can be done, as we did in later studies on addiction and migration (see Flick and Röhnsch, 2014) and migration and unemployment (see Flick et al., 2017).

SITUATIONAL ANALYSIS

Clarke (2005) goes in a different direction with her approach of situational analysis. She picks up parts of Strauss and Corbin's (1990) version of grounded theory coding, when she directly refers to the conditional matrix these authors suggested (see Chapter 4). Clarke also engages in connecting grounded theory as a research programme with newer developments in the social sciences, as 'situational analysis allows researchers to draw together studies of discourse and agency, action and structure, image, text and context, history and the present moment' (Clarke, 2005, p. xxii). Clarke emphasizes her difference to grounded theory research according to Glaser (heading for 'basic social process'), and connects with other aspects in Strauss's situation-centred 'social worlds/arenas/negotiations' framework approach. However, Clarke demonstrates at several points in her book that she uses grounded theory coding in her studies, even if she does not describe or reformulate coding or coding procedures in detail. For narrative materials, she suggests: 'As with mapping interview and fieldwork data, basic grounded theory coding of the narrative materials should be pursued first' (Clarke, 2005, p. 187). She continuously draws strong links to Strauss in outlining her method and the methodological contribution of situational analysis, which focuses on cartographic approaches to drawing situational maps (to better understand the research situation), social worlds and arena maps (addressing collective actors and discourses), and positional maps showing which positions are taken by the actors that are involved (see Box 5.4).

BOX 5.4   SITUATIONAL ANALYSIS AND GROUNDED THEORY

Building upon and extending Strauss's work, situational analysis offers three main cartographic approaches:

1. Situational maps that lay out the major human, nonhuman, discursive and other elements in the research situation of inquiry and provoke analysis of relations among them.
2. Social worlds/arenas maps that lay out the collective actors, key nonhuman elements, and the arena(s) of commitment and discourse within which they are engaged in ongoing negotiations – meso-level interpretations of the situation.
3. Positional maps that lay out the major positions taken, and not taken, in the data vis-à-vis particular axes of difference, concern and controversy around issues in the situation of inquiry.

(Clarke, 2005, p. xxii)

The use of maps as a methodological tool is outlined at a later point in her book. The main shift from grounded theory in Glaser and Strauss (1967) to situational analysis in Clarke (2005) is that the emergence of a basic social process or of an underlying paradigm is no longer the focus of her research. Clarke (2005, pp. 11–12) sees a number of shortcomings in traditional grounded theory that have to be overcome in this shift in the methodology, among them a lack of reflexivity about research processes, oversimplifications aiming at coherence and a singular social process, and the search for purity in grounded theory research. Instead, Clarke is interested in drawing maps of more or less complex situations in which phenomena become relevant. For identifying what is relevant for understanding a situation, Clarke still uses coding procedures in the sense of Glaser, Strauss, Corbin and Charmaz but puts much more emphasis on understanding social relations and structures by representing (mapping) them or what characterizes these situations. Her focus is on increasingly complex situations and their mapping, beginning from actual situations (in which participants communicate and have a specific, e.g. client–consumer, relation). This approach extends to social worlds, where no longer do only individual actors communicate, but collectivities and relations beyond the concrete situations are at stake and finally in process, such as discourses acting on what individuals or members of social worlds do consciously or unconsciously (see Box 5.5)

BOX 5.5   TYPES OF SITUATIONAL MAPS AND ANALYSES

There are three main types of **situational maps and analyses**:

1.   **Situational maps** as strategies for articulating the elements in the situation and examining relations among them.
2.   **Social worlds/arenas maps** as cartographies of collective commitments, relations, and sites of action.
3.   **Positional maps** as simplification strategies for plotting positions articulated and not articulated in discourses.

(Clarke, 2005, p. 86, original emphasis)

These extensions of what is in the focus of grounded theory are not just extensions of what is studied, or how data are collected or analyzed in the context of grounded theory research. They also reposition grounded theory research – and the way it articulates and analyzes issues in the empirical focus – in a fundamental way. Grounded theory research in Clarke's versions is 'suddenly' located – 'being pushed and pulled' – around the postmodern turn. Clarke's programme of reformulating grounded theory in a postmodern version and of revising its methodological approach to phenomena under study is far-reaching in reformulating and extending the issues (i.e. social arenas) to be studied, the methods that are used (mapping and analyzing situations) and the outcome to be expected (sensitizing concepts instead of substantive theories).

DIFFERENCES AND COMMON ASPECTS: IDENTIFYING STRUCTURE AND REDUCING COMPLEXITY

The aims of coding in the processes in the various approaches outlined in this and the preceding chapter are always twofold. After developing and unfolding an understanding of the issue or field under study, which demands open access to what should be coded and how, an underlying structure, an organizing principle, a basic social process or core category shall be identified. This asks for reduction and structuration. Glaser's (1978) distinction between substantive and theoretical coding aims at realizing both of these aims. Therefore he suggests using either words and concepts from the language of the field ('*in vivo* codes'), or words and concepts drawn from the scientific (e.g. sociological) terminology ('sociological constructs'). Theoretical coding then aims at identifying relations among such substantive codes as the next step towards formulating a theory. Here we find suggestions to look for relations among codes like causes, contexts, consequences and conditions (1978, p. 72). The same applies to the coding 'families' Glaser suggests.

In Strauss's concept of coding, the coding paradigm (or paradigmatic model) is the equivalent to the coding families in Glaser's approach. Here again an orientation is given for how to link substantive concepts with each other. Again this is an abstract and general model for how to link and contextualize substantive codes among each other. This model is constructed around two axes: one goes from causes to phenomena and to consequences, the other goes from context to intervening conditions and to action and interactional strategies of participants. Accordingly you may take a phenomenon, which was labelled with a substantive code, and ask yourself along the first axis: what are the causes of this phenomenon and what are its consequences? On the second axis you may ask: what were the context and intervening conditions influencing this phenomenon, which strategies by participants were linked to this phenomenon, and what were the consequences? Of course these questions are not hypothetical but should be addressed to the empirical material and answered by coding and comparison.

In both approaches, substantive codes are linked by codes that are more about formal relations (something is a *cause* of something). Strauss's model around two axes led to his step of axial coding, which takes this model as a heuristic device for further developing a grounded theory. In both approaches, the idea of selective coding is included, which focuses on potential core concepts or core variables (Holton, 2007, p. 280). Also, constant comparison of materials during the coding process is beyond question for both approaches. Integration of materials and developing the structure of the theory are advanced by the theoretical sorting of codes and even more by memos written about them. Several authors suggest doing this sorting by hand. The theoretical codes produced in one of the ways discussed above can be used as an orientation for theoretical sorting (see Charmaz, 2014, pp. 216–18). In general, the alternatives outlined for applying grounded theory coding are different routes to the same aim. Strauss and Corbin have focused their approach to material more on a basic model (paradigm model) with a limited number of elements and links between them. Glaser has developed a broader set of basic ways of coding (coding families) from his experiences. Charmaz has developed that into a more constructivist approach to materials and to theories. This affects epistemological issues as well ('Finding or constructing theories?') whereas the distinction between Strauss's and Glaser's approaches is substantially based on how strict and how open the researcher's own approach to data is. Glaser may be more flexible here and less oriented on traditional models of science (the use of 'paradigm' and the criteria suggested by Strauss and Corbin – see Chapters 4 and 7 – may support this notion) but tends at some points to over-emphasize his notion of flexibility in his approach to material (formulations like 'All is data' and 'Just do it' characterize some of his later writings, e.g. Glaser, 2002). For your own research, you should look at the tools each approach suggests for analyzing material, and see which fits best for your own material and attitude towards it. Beyond the disputes between Glaser and Strauss and Corbin, the more current suggestions of Charmaz (e.g. Thornberg and Charmaz, 2014) point the way for the future development of grounded theory coding.

CONCLUSION

What do we find in the recent developments presented in this chapter? We see, in Charmaz's approach, an attempt to first outline a more contemporary (constructivist) conceptualization of grounded theory coding and research in general with two more aims. First, to keep this programme a practical and pragmatic way of doing qualitative (grounded theory) research, and as a second aim the pacification of the not always pleasant battles among the developmental positions within grounded theory discourse and with critics from outside. In Holton and Walsh's approach we see a continuation of one of these developmental positions (Glaserian classic grounded theory) with some extensions (to latent patterns) and clarification of this specific approach. In the suggestion of case-oriented thematic coding, we see an attempt to make grounded theory analysis work in studies focusing on individuals (e.g. interviewees) as cases and on the differences and commonalities among them. In situational analysis, finally, we find a fundamental re-orientation of grounded theory research (from basic processes to social maps) practically based on earlier versions, but embedded in a much wider epistemological shift and extension to postmodern views of knowledge, social worlds and practices. These developments make the procedures of data analysis more concrete at some points and add new approaches to data and phenomena to the tool box of grounded theory coding and research.

● KEY POINTS

- Charmaz's approach to grounded theory provides a mild modernization of grounded theory research as a constructivist programme. This includes concrete and orienting suggestions for how to code.
- Holton and Walsh update Glaser's classic grounded theory approach and refocus his analysis on data in some ways.
- Thematic coding is a suggestion for a stronger orientation on participants as cases.
- Situational analysis takes a more radical re-orientation of grounded theory research on an epistemological level as well as what the empirical research is about.

■ FURTHER READING

Constructivist grounded theory and its practicalities are spelled out in more detail in the following sources:

Bryant, A. and Charmaz, K. (eds) (2007) *The SAGE Handbook of Grounded Theory*. London: Sage.

Charmaz, K. (2014) *Constructing Grounded Theory: A Practical Guide through Qualitative Analysis*. London: Sage.

Thornberg, R. and Charmaz, K. (2014) 'Grounded theory and theoretical coding', in U. Flick (ed.), *The SAGE Handbook of Qualitative Data Analysis*. London: Sage, pp. 153–69.

Situational analysis and its practicalities are unfolded in more detail in:

Clarke, A. (2005) *Situational Analysis. Grounded Theory after the Postmodern Turn*. Thousand Oaks, CA: Sage.

Classic grounded theory is presented in detail in this book:

Holton, J.A. and Walsh, I. (2017) *Classic Grounded Theory – Applications with Qualitative and Quantitative Data*. London: Sage.

Qualitative data analysis in general and by using CAQDAS software is covered in:

Gibbs, G.R. (2018) *Analyzing Qualitative Data* (Book 6 of *The SAGE Qualitative Research Kit*, 2nd ed.). London: Sage.

CHAPTER SIX

GOING BEYOND

THEORETICAL SAMPLING, SATURATION AND SORTING

CONTENTS

CHAPTER OBJECTIVES

After reading this chapter, you should have understood:

- what defines theoretical sampling and distinguishes it from other forms of sampling;
- what characterizes theoretical saturation and how to use it in research; and
- what theoretical sorting means.

In this chapter, some of the key concepts in doing grounded theory are discussed. Their centrality varies among the different versions of grounded theory research, but they are seen as characteristics of grounded theory as a whole (see Chapters 1 and 2). We will begin with theoretical sampling as one of the most important features of this kind of research. It may be a bit surprising that this is introduced in this book only after describing data collection and data analysis in detail. However, there are some reasons for this structure, which result from the differences between sampling in quantitative and in qualitative research, and between sampling in both and grounded theory sampling.

THEORETICAL SAMPLING

It might be helpful to recall the main concepts of sampling for a better understanding of theoretical sampling.

Current understandings of sampling

Sampling in quantitative research is the step before data collection, which aims at representing the structure of a bigger population in the sample that is actually studied. This should allow us to generalize the results from the study to a population bigger than the group that has been selected for doing the study. In qualitative research, sampling is not so much about finding the best cases to represent the bigger population, but to find the right cases for doing informative interviews or observations, for example. Morse (2007) has formulated a number of principles of sampling for all qualitative inquiry (2007, p. 229–34) including 'It is necessary to locate "excellent" participants to obtain excellent data'. This refers to finding those people who know best about an issue or can give you the best insights, but also to finding the best situations where you can observe what is relevant for your studies. Here, an earlier distinction Morse (1998) suggested becomes relevant. The 'primary selection' includes those who optimally meet your criteria of knowledge about an issue and skills of talking about it in an instructive way. The 'secondary selection' includes those who have less knowledge and skills but are ready to participate in the study. You should take care to have only or mainly the first group in the sample. Sampling should focus on specific participants (or situations) who are most informative and not include whoever might be interested or interesting.

Sampling in grounded theory

In grounded theory research, sampling is not driven by the logic of substitution and generalization we find in quantitative research. Theoretical sampling is more than such a selection.

The original concept of theoretical sampling

As we saw in Chapter 3, Glaser and Strauss (1967) did not include a specific chapter on data collection (methods) in their book but treated data collection as a topic in their outline of theoretical sampling. Decisions about choosing and putting together empirical material (cases, groups, institutions, etc.) are made in the process of collecting and interpreting data. Glaser and Strauss describe this strategy as that the researcher 'jointly collects, codes, and analyzes his data and decides what data to collect next and where to find them' (1967, p. 45). Sampling decisions in theoretical sampling may start from either of two levels: you may take them on the level of the groups to be compared or they may directly focus on specific persons. In both cases, the sampling of concrete individuals, groups or fields is not based on the usual criteria and techniques of statistical sampling. You would employ neither random sampling nor stratification to make a sample representative. Rather, you would select individuals, groups, and so on according to their (expected) level of new insights for the developing theory in relation to the state of theory elaboration so far. Sampling decisions aim at the material that promises the greatest insights, viewed in the light of the material already used, and the knowledge drawn from it. The main questions for selecting data are: 'What groups or subgroups does one turn to next in data collection? And for what theoretical purpose?' (1967, p. 47).

Given the theoretically unlimited possibilities of integrating further persons, groups, cases, and so on it is necessary to define criteria for a well-founded limitation of the sampling. These criteria are defined here in relation to the theory. The theory developing from the empirical material is the point of reference. Examples of such criteria are how promising the next case is and how relevant it might be for developing the theory.

An example of applying this form of sampling can be found in Glaser and Strauss's (1965a) study on awareness of dying in hospitals. In this study, the authors did participant observation in different hospitals in order to develop a theory about how dying in hospital is organized as a social process (see Box 6.1, and also Case studies 1.1 and 2.1 for more details).

BOX 6.1   EXAMPLE OF THEORETICAL SAMPLING

Glaser and Strauss describe in the following passage how they proceeded in theoretical sampling:

> Visits to the various medical services were scheduled as follows. I wished first to look at services that minimized patient awareness (and so first looked at a premature baby service and then at a neurosurgical service where patients were frequently comatose). Next I wished to look at the dying in a situation where expectancy of staff and often of patients was great and dying was quick, so I observed on an Intensive Care Unit. Then I wished to observe on a service where staff expectations of terminality were great but where the patient's might or might not be, and where dying tended to be slow. So I looked next at a cancer service. I wished then to look at conditions where death was unexpected and rapid, and so looked at an emergency service. While we were looking at some different types of services, we also observed the above types of services at other types of hospitals. So our scheduling of types of service was directed by a general conceptual scheme – which included hypotheses about awareness, expectedness, and rate of dying – as well as by a developing conceptual structure including matters not at first envisioned. Sometimes we returned to services after the initial two or three or four weeks of continuous observation, in order to check upon items which needed checking or had been missed in the initial period.

(Glaser and Strauss, 1967, p. 59)

Further elaboration of theoretical sampling

This example is instructive as it shows how, in constructing their sample, the researchers went step by step in their contact with the field while they collected their data.

In their later elaboration of Strauss's approach, Strauss and Corbin (1990) spelled out theoretical sampling in more detail. First they highlight that they refer to sampling events, incidents but not persons (1990, p. 177). They continue by making suggestions for sampling in each of the coding procedures in their approach. In open coding, sampling can be based on (1) *purposefully* looking 'for data bearing on categories, their properties, and dimensions' (p. 183). (2) You may proceed very systematically based on a list of properties to include. (3) Data are often 'bearing upon open sampling ... [and] emerge fortuitously' (1990, p. 184). In the context of axial coding, sampling is relational (according to the coding paradigm – see Chapter 4) and variational, aiming at finding 'as many differences as possible at the dimensional level in the data' (1990, p. 185). In selective coding, 'discriminate sampling' is applied in order to 'maximize opportunities for verifying the story line, relationships between categories, and for filing in poorly developed categories' (1990, p. 187).

The current concepts of theoretical sampling

Charmaz (2014) underlines that the wider understanding of the relevance of theoretical sampling originally outlined by Glaser and Strauss (1967) and Strauss and Corbin (1990) is still shared in grounded theory methodology discourse. One of the main differences from sampling in other forms of qualitative research is that theoretical sampling does not occur on the way to the data (which interviewee to select) but on the way from the data to the theory. It does not refer to where to start the research (with whom or in which situations to collect the first data) but to how to elaborate and consolidate the theory that is developing; see Box 6.2).

BOX 6.2 WHAT THEORETICAL SAMPLING IS NOT

Sometimes qualitative researchers claim to use theoretical sampling but do not follow the logic of grounded theory. They mistake theoretical sampling for the following types of sampling:

- Sampling to address initial research questions.
- Sampling to reflect population distributions.
- Sampling to find negative cases.
- Sampling until no new data emerge. (Charmaz, 2014, p. 197)

Thus, theoretical sampling does not refer to the first research questions, or population distributions, looking for negative cases or to the point where no new data can be found (Charmaz, 2014, p. 197).

Theoretical sampling does not refer to decisions about individuals (who should be the next interviewee?) but to properties of the first or developing categories: 'Theoretical sampling pertains only to conceptual and theoretical development of your analysis; it is not about representing a population or increasing the statistical generalizability of your results' (Charmaz, 2014, p. 198). Thus, before sampling can become *theoretical* sampling, first data and first analyses must have led to first categories at least, so that you can use theoretical sampling for elaborating and refining theoretical categories.

Although Charmaz discusses in great detail specific methods of data collection in her book, she sticks to the idea that theoretical sampling is the main principle and method to use for producing the data you need to consolidate your categories and/ or theories. This specific subordination of methods under specific needs of theoretical sampling remains part of the current version of grounded theory methodology. There are also various tasks for which theoretical sampling is the tool in the process of the research such as to help 'to check, qualify, and elaborate the boundaries of your categories and to specify the relations among categories' (2014, p. 205).

Abduction as a principle in theoretical sampling

In constructivist grounded theory, abduction (see Chapter 1) plays a major role for several of the elements in the research process. Among them is theoretical sampling, as Charmaz emphasizes in several publications. She also sees the special characteristics of theoretical sampling in distinction to other forms of sampling in its close link to abductive reasoning, which is a distinctive feature of grounded theory. One of the main advances in using abductive reasoning is that it opens up more space for the intended interaction between the researchers and their data, between the researchers and their theory fragments so far developed, and between their data and theory. In particular the decision about whom or what to include next in the theoretical sampling process on the basis of the data and their analysis so far reaches beyond pure induction or a more or less formal deduction. Here, you have to interpret, evaluate and perhaps reread your data and interpretations and to develop creativity in taking decisions.

In theoretical sampling, decisions are often based on tentative and hypothetical reasoning, as they are driven by the expectations about what the new case or group will contribute to developing the categories or theory. Thornberg and Charmaz (2014) underline that abductive reasoning – in contrast to pure induction – is based on existing theoretical knowledge and on interpretive actions by the researchers. It has a lot to do with creativity in linking back the state of the developing theory to the potentialities in the field under study – where to look and search next for further data and insights for the theory underway. All in all, the suggestions for doing theoretical sampling can be summarized in a number of purposes such as delineating categories and saturating their properties and clarifying relations between categories – see Box 6.3.

BOX 6.3 PURPOSES OF THEORETICAL SAMPLING

Use theoretical sampling to keep you moving toward such emergent objectives as:

- To delineate the properties of a category.
- To check hunches about categories.
- To saturate the properties of a category.
- To distinguish between categories.
- To clarify relationships between emerging categories.
- To identify variation in a process.

(Charmaz, 2014, p. 232)

Lastly, Morse (2007, pp. 234–41) integrates her discussion of sampling in qualitative inquiry and in grounded theory in a model consisting of four stages. The first stage is convenience sampling, which means (first) participants or situations are selected on the basis of accessibility. The second stage is to use purposeful sampling: participants selected as indicated by the initial analysis of interviews. Here, the suggestions made by Patton (2015; see also Flick, 2018c, Chapter 4) can give a helpful orientation. He suggests: (1) integrating purposively *extreme* or deviant cases; (2) selecting particularly *typical* cases; (3) aiming at *maximal variation* in the sample; (4) purposive sampling according to the *intensity* with which the interesting features, processes, experiences, and so on are given or assumed in them; (5) sampling *critical cases* aimed at those cases in which the relations to be studied become especially clear. The third stage in Morse's (2007) model refers to theoretical sampling, when participants are selected according to the descriptive needs of emerging concepts and theory. As a fourth stage she suggests doing theoretical group interviews to expand and verify the emerging model.

Problems of theoretical sampling

Theoretical sampling is an essential of grounded theory methodology. If it is applied consistently as the strategy leading to the empirical material used for elaborating the categories and the theory in the end, it makes the methodology of a grounded theory study really sophisticated. However, this strategy may lead to a number of problems. First of all, theoretical sampling can be located too early in the process and then lead to problems, such as premature closure of analytic categories, redundant categories, over-reliance on overt statements and unfocused or unspecified categories.

Another problem may arise in contexts, where it is (seen as) necessary that you define and outline in advance what you will really do in your study. This can be the case if a study needs external funding and a calculation of the costs to be expected in a grant proposal as well as the time needed for doing the study. A second context is the institutional review boards assessing the relevance and ethical legitimacy of what you will do in a field or with participants. Again this may be difficult to define in advance if theoretical sampling is taken seriously. And finally, sampling is always the plan of whom or what to integrate in a study at a certain point. Whether or not this plan works, and the individuals, incidents or situations necessary for elaborating a developed category are found, is a question of access – to fields, to members, to documents and the like (see Flick, 2018c, Chapter 4).

THEORETICAL SATURATION

Very briefly summarized, the process of discovery moves along the path from initial sampling and data collection; open coding; theoretical sampling; collecting more data; axial, focused, theoretical and selective coding; theoretical sampling again; collecting more data; axial, focused, theoretical and selective coding. It reaches its aim when theoretical saturation has been accomplished. This is another of the essential but often a bit mysterious concepts in grounded theory research. What is theoretical saturation? Bryant and Charmaz (2007b, p. 611) provide as a current and general definition, that it means the point where new data neither provide new properties of a category nor further insights about the theory. When Glaser and Strauss (1967) originally introduced this concept in their approach, it was closely linked to theoretical sampling and defined as a criterion seeing sampling as completed, in particular when similar instances can be seen repeatedly. That a category is saturated, however, is something researchers become confident about and not something defined in a systematic way. Theoretical saturation also becomes the point of reference for judging the exhaustiveness with which categories have been developed. For Glaser, in his later works (2001, p. 192) it is also a criterion for judging theoretical completeness. He also underlines that it is not repetition and similarity which define saturation but variation, which is becoming evident in comparison, that indicates that saturation has been reached. But how to judge whether the state of theoretical saturation has been reached? Glaser and Strauss (1967) already saw the problem of an empirical escapism, which means that the researchers tend to continue endlessly with sampling and collecting new data instead of staying closer to existing categories and deciding whether theoretical saturation has been reached (or not).

A number of issues are related to this concept on a practical level. The first is that sometimes the important specification of saturation to be 'theoretical' is omitted. Saturation does not mean that there are no more data to collect, no more cases to be included, no more interviews to be done. It only means that more data are no longer necessary for developing an existing (i.e. already developed) category. So the link between saturation and the decision of when to stop sampling and collecting data always takes the route along the concepts and relations developed so far. This makes it difficult to define theoretical saturation in a simple way in terms of when it is reached and how to apply it. Another problem is that neither deduction nor induction allow us to answer the question of 'Has theoretical saturation been reached?', but it is rather one of the moments in the process where abduction becomes relevant. Finally, there are differences in the way the various approaches in grounded theory make use of this concept. Charmaz (2014) sees it as a strongly abductive reasoning problem. Clarke (2005) uses the concept of 'saturation' for deciding whether a situational or positional map is complete, but no longer links it to 'theory'. Glaser (2001) sees theoretical saturation as an issue which is relevant for several steps – in developing categories, in theoretical coding, in the developing of the theory as such. This means it becomes relevant before and after theoretical sorting, which will be discussed next.

THEORETICAL SORTING

The idea that sorting of materials, memos and categories will be a major contribution to theory development was introduced by Glaser (1978) but not taken up in the further development of the methodology by Strauss and Corbin. Interestingly enough, Glaser locates this step after the saturation of categories and mainly in the stage when the researchers begin to write up their theory. This concept has been maintained and reactivated in classic grounded theory by Holton and Walsh (2017) but also by Charmaz (2014, p. 236). Glaser had suggested a number of analytic rules (see a current version in Holton and Walsh, 2017, p. 115–16). Sorting should start anywhere in the process, be related to the core variable (core category, basic social process), promote or demote core variables, and include constant memoing. It should carry the analyst forward, have an integrative fit, address two levels (core category and subcategories, for example), and force the analyst toward new ideas. Sorting should be oriented on cutting-off rules (e.g. theoretical completeness and coverage), and lead to theory development (theoretical pacing). An interesting emphasis was introduced by Glaser, but is maintained by Holton and Walsh with an insistence on handsorting of memos, which makes the analyst discriminate the fit of ideas in the developing theory: the 'physical act of handsorting memos further facilitates the preconscious processing of matured ideas' (2017, p. 109). This is an interesting insistence in times when qualitative data analysis often proceeds using CAQDAS programmes (see Gibbs, 2018). It may be a reaction to the fact that the Strauss and Corbin approach to grounded theory data analysis was the model for developing programmes such as ATLAS.ti. It may also be read as a reaction to the development that the idea of theoretical sorting was driven into the background by the emphasis on diagramming the developmental state of a developing theory in Strauss and Corbin's, Clarke's and Charmaz's approaches. Charmaz (2014, p. 238) gives some advice on how to do theoretical sorting (see Box 6.4).

BOX 6.4   ADVICE FOR DOING THEORETICAL SORTING

- Sort memos by the title of each category.
- Compare categories.
- Use your categories carefully.
- Consider how their order reflects the studied experience.
- Now think how their order fits the logic of the categories.
- Create the best possible balance between the studied experience, your categories, and your theoretical statements about them.

(Charmaz, 2014, p. 238)

The concept of theoretical sorting in Glaser's formulations as well as in Charmaz's description links the analysis of data and the development of theory very closely to writing up the theory and writing in the process.

● KEY POINTS

- Theoretical sampling is a key concept in grounded theory methodology.
- It is different from other forms of sampling in qualitative or quantitative research.
- Theoretical saturation refers to the sufficient elaboration of categories and of the theory, but not to the end of possible data collection.
- Theoretical sorting can be seen as a way of bringing structure into the developing categories and the theory, and in particular among the memos that have been written.

■ FURTHER READING

These procedures for advancing coding and theory development are further elaborated in the following works:

Charmaz, K. (2014) *Constructing Grounded Theory: A Practical Guide through Qualitative Analysis*. London: Sage.

Gibbs, G.R. (2018) *Analyzing Qualitative Data* (Book 6 of *The SAGE Qualitative Research Kit*, 2nd ed.). London: Sage.

Glaser, B.G. and Strauss, A.L. (1967) *The Discovery of Grounded Theory: Strategies for Qualitative Research*. Chicago: Aldine.

Holton, J.A. and Walsh, I. (2017*) Classic Grounded Theory – Applications with Qualitative and Quantitative Data*. London: Sage.

Thornberg, R. and Charmaz, K. (2014) 'Grounded theory and theoretical coding', in U. Flick (ed.), *The SAGE Handbook of Qualitative Data Analysis*. London: Sage, pp. 153–69.

CHAPTER SEVEN

OUTPUT
WRITING AND QUALITY IN GROUNDED THEORY

CONTENTS

CHAPTER OBJECTIVES

After reading this chapter, you should understand:

- the role of writing in the grounded theory research process;
- the importance of writing memos in the research and for writing about it;
- the various suggestions for criteria in versions of grounded theory; and
- ways of evaluating process and outcomes in grounded theory research.

In a grounded theory project, as in every other form of research, you are confronted with two challenges on the level of outcome. First, to document what came out of the whole project, how this was achieved and to publish it somewhere so that results become accessible. Second, you need to demonstrate that your research and your findings are good examples of research and sustainable in the light of scientific standards. Thus, the issue of writing comes to the fore in two respects.

First, in the social sciences, text is not only an instrument for documenting data and a basis for interpretation and thus an epistemological instrument, but also an instrument of mediating and communicating findings and knowledge. Sometimes writing is even seen as the core of social science: 'To do social science means mainly to produce texts … A research process has findings only when and as far as these can be found in a report' (Wolff, 1987, p. 333).

Second, writing provides the material for a critical assessment of what you did, how you did it and what came out. The critical assessment of these aspects – by the researchers for their own project and for other researchers, peer reviewers, users of findings, etc. – is often linked to criteria. In the grounded theory literature, the issue of appropriate criteria has been a prominent topic from the beginning to more recent publications and the second part of this chapter will discuss the suggestions that have been made. Writing in grounded theory is not only seen as publishing the results but also as an essential element in the research process, which will be outlined in the first part of the chapter.

WRITING IN GROUNDED THEORY THROUGHOUT THE PROCESS

Memo writing

Writing becomes relevant in two stages of the process. Before writing publications, reports and results towards the end it also is a main activity in doing the research, in particular in writing memos as an essential of grounded theory research practice

(Lempert, 2007, p. 245). This highlights the central role of writing in the process of theory development. However, most theorists of grounded theory methodology locate memo writing essentially in the step of analyzing the data: memos are less intended to contain descriptions of the setting that is studied but should '*conceptualize* the data in narrative form' (2007, p. 245). Memo writing can include references to the literature and diagrams to link, structure and contextualize concepts. Memos may also incorporate quotes from respondents in interviews or field conversations as further evidence in the analysis.

Memoing is not a standardized procedure but depends on the personal style of the researcher. However, it can be seen as a learned skill. Lempert sees four fundamental principles in memo writing. The intention is the discovery (1) and development of theory rather than application and confirmation. A major step in analyzing any sort of raw data is memo writing and diagramming of concepts (2), both of which help to shape the further collection and analysis of data (3). Memos are written, reread and rewritten (4) in order to advance to more abstract levels of theorizing (2007, p. 262).

Memo writing helps to make the analysis more explicit and transparent for the researcher, for other people in the team, and, if used as part of a publication, for readers of the research and its results. However, a consistent use of memoing should go beyond analyzing data. The research will benefit a lot if memo writing starts right away with writing a research diary throughout the process. Writing field notes should complement this once you get in touch with your empirical area and the members of the field. If you do interviews, you should write an extended context protocol including impressions, descriptions of the setting in which an interview was done, circumstances and intriguing events in your relation to the field and the interviewee. This protocol complements the recording and **transcription** of what has been said in the interview. In general, you should try to make notes throughout the process of your research.

Memos – types and functions

Richardson (1994, p. 527) distinguishes four categories of notes that are helpful for documenting and reflecting on the process of research: observational, methodological, theoretical and personal notes. This extension of memoing will make evident how your research advanced and how you produced evidence that allowed construction of your theory in the process. Gibbs (2018, p. 45–6) adds as reasons for memoing during analysis: (1) a new idea for a code; (2) just a quick hunch about what is supported by evidence in the data; (3) integrative discussion (e.g. of previous reflective remarks); (4) as a dialogue amongst researchers.

Writing in the process – discovery through writing

In grounded theory research, writing is not limited to taking notes in memos or presenting the outcome of the research at the end. Charmaz highlights the central role of writing in the research process as a source of findings in the analysis, which should complement and ground the development of categories and theory elements as 'writing and rewriting become crucial phases of the *analytic* process' (Charmaz, 2014, p. 289).

If we take this suggestion seriously, the benefit of writing during and as an analytic tool comes from writing and rewriting drafts of argumentations, of analyses and interpretations.

Sorting, selective coding and diagramming

In Chapter 6, it was mentioned that later stages in the analysis, such as theoretical sorting in Glaser's (1978) version of grounded theory research, directly lead to writing the theory and have become part of this. Strauss and Corbin's (1990) concept of selective coding is strongly oriented to writing the story and later the story line of the case. Starting with their approach, the function of diagramming has become a major tool for clarifying the theory (or intermediate steps of its development). Examples are the conditional matrix they suggested as a way of structuring and contextualizing phenomena that are studied or the various forms of mapping that are part of Clarke's situational analysis (2005). Finally, the appeal of CAQDAS software packages such as ATLAS.ti or **MAXQDA** (see Gibbs, 2018) has to do with the ways of displaying categories, relations between categories or links to data excerpts in diagrams. As Glaser and Strauss mentioned very early on, writing, memoing, displaying connections and the like are closely linked (1967, p. 113).

PRESENTATION OF GROUNDED THEORIES

The outcome of a grounded theory project should be a theory, but this may not always be the case. Often interesting data and analysis are elaborated to interesting results but not necessarily to a theory, as in the example of Glaser and Strauss (1965a). The presentation of such a theory requires, according to Strauss and Corbin (1990, p. 229):

(1) A clear analytic story. (2) Writing on a conceptual level, with description kept secondary. (3) The clear specification of relationships among categories, with levels of conceptualization also kept clear. (4) The specification of variations and their relevant conditions, consequences, and so forth, including the broader ones.

Lofland's suggestions for presenting findings in the form of theories head in a similar direction. He mentions as criteria for writing the same criteria as for evaluating such reports (1974, p. 102), namely ensuring that a theoretical framework structures the text, that new aspects characterize this framework and that data and empirical material substantiate the report.

Writing grounded theory or writing in social sciences in general?

Writing is seen as an essential part of doing grounded theory. This is also documented in most textbooks (e.g. Charmaz, 2014; Corbin and Strauss, 2015; Holton and Walsh, 2017) which include long sections on writing. However, most of these sections mainly give general advice about what to consider in scientific writing, in completing a thesis or in submitting an article. Less detailed in these sections is the specific challenge of writing about theory development. Writing the theory and about the process that led to developing it makes the outcome of a grounded theory project accessible, available and accountable concerning the quality of the research.

GROUNDING GROUNDED THEORY – HOW TO ASSESS THE QUALITY

Starting points – Glaser and Strauss's concept

How to assess the quality of grounded theory was an issue for Glaser and Strauss even before their textbook was published, when they raised doubts as to the applicability of the canons of quantitative research as criteria for judging the credibility of substantive theory based on qualitative research. They suggested rather that judgement criteria be based on generic elements of qualitative methods for collecting, analyzing and presenting data and for the way in which people read qualitative analyses (1965b, p. 5).

The quality question can be asked on three levels in doing grounded theory:

- About the way the research was done, how methods or sampling were applied, for example.
- About the results the research produced, in particular whether the results should be a theory.
- And finally, how transparent the theory, as well as the research that lead to it, became in the researchers' presentation.

In their original book, Glaser and Strauss (1967) addressed the question of criteria for judging grounded theory research from two angles. For the first level mentioned above, they defined a number of criteria for judging how the research was done in each phase (collecting or analyzing data, for example). These research- and analysis-oriented criteria are the first angle from which they deal with the quality of grounded theory research. But at the same time, Glaser and Strauss (1967) had a specific kind of theory in mind, which is not an abstract general theory developed on a theoretical level, but a theory that can be applied for solving specific problems and also be understandable in contexts beyond theoretical sociology. Therefore, a grounded theory must 'closely fit' the substantive area and be readily understandable for lay-people in this area. Furthermore, it must be general enough that it can be applied to various daily situations in this area and allow the user control of the structure and process of daily situations (see Glaser and Strauss, 1967, p. 237). In later work, Glaser and Strauss (1971) provided more details about their ideas: grounded theory means a 'theory that fits the real world, works in predictions and explanations, is relevant for the people concerned and ... is readily modifiable' (p. 176), and this can again be found in Glaser (1978, pp. 4–5).

Proliferations: Glaser's reading of relevance and quality

Glaser (1998, pp. 18–19) later detailed and specified these criteria by emphasizing the fit (i.e. **validity**), the workability (i.e. explanatory potential), the relevance (for the participants), and the modifiability of the theory (by new data for example – see Box 7.1).

BOX 7.1   CRITERIA FOR CLASSIC GROUNDED THEORY

1. Fit is another word for validity. Does the concept adequately express the pattern in the data which it purports to conceptualize? Fit is continually sharpened by constant comparison.
2. Workability means do the concepts and the way they are related into hypotheses sufficiently account for how the main concern of the participants in a substantive area is continuously resolved?
3. Relevance makes the research important, because it deals with the main concerns of the participants involved. To study something that interests no one really or just a few academics or funders is probably to focus on non-relevance or even trivia for the participants. Relevance, like good concepts, evokes instant grab.

4. Modifiability is very significant. The theory is not being verified as in verification studies, and thus never right or wrong ... it just gets modified by new data to compare it to ... New data never provides a disproof, just an analytic challenge.

(Glaser, 1998, p. 18–19).

These elaborations of the original criteria by Glaser, however, reveal a very participant-oriented attitude, when relevance is only seen from their perspective and not from other points of reference. The same applies to the fourth criterion, when a very particular idea of the role of theories in social sciences is revealed. On the one hand, it is **falsification** rather than verification that Glaser refers to when he distinguishes grounded theory from other theories. On the other hand, he essentially excludes the idea that a theory could be wrong or inadequate or questioned by new insights. Whatever the basic idea behind these four criteria, Glaser's later reading reveals an anti-scientific approach to the evaluation of (grounded theory) research. Holton and Walsh (2017) add the criteria of 'logical consistency, clarity, parsimony, density, scope (and) integration' from Glaser and Strauss's (1967, p. 3) original outline. They link this to more general reflection on what a good grounded theory is like from Eisenstadt (1989), who mentions four main qualities. A good theory coming out of this process should be parsimonious, testable and logically coherent, and include new insights (1989, p. 548).

Strauss and Corbin: quality of grounded theories in a scientific context

Strauss and Corbin go in a different direction, when they (1990, p. 16) mention four points of departure for judging empirically grounded theories and the procedures that led to them. According to their suggestion, you should critically assess: (1) the validity, reliability, and credibility of the data; (2) the plausibility, and the value of the theory itself; (3) the adequacy of the research process which has generated, elaborated, or tested the theory; and (4) the empirical grounding of the research findings.

In this outline, we find an attempt at combining the general criteria for assessing research, that were originally rejected by Glaser and Strauss (e.g. validity), and new and specific grounded theory criteria (empirical grounding and value of the theory). For evaluating the research process itself, Strauss and Corbin suggest seven criteria referring to how the sampling was done, which categories emerged, how these are grounded in events or incidents, how analysis informed theoretical sampling, which hypotheses about relations between categories were developed and tested. These criteria also refer to which discrepancies became visible and how they were treated, and finally how the core category was identified (see Corbin and Strauss, 1990, p. 17).

The evaluation of theory development ends up by answering the question of how far the concepts – such as theoretical sampling and the different forms of coding – in Strauss's approach were applied and whether this application corresponds with the methodological ideas of the authors. Thus efforts to evaluate proceedings and findings remain within the framework of their own system.

A central role is given to the question of whether the findings and the theory are grounded in the empirical relations and data – whether it is a grounded theory (building) or not. For an evaluation of the realization of this aim, Corbin and Strauss suggest another seven criteria for answering the question of the empirical grounding of findings and theories. These focus on the concepts and whether their links are well developed, on variations and conditions, and on considering process and significance of the findings (1990, pp. 17–18).

The point of reference, here again, is the procedure formulated by the authors and whether it has been applied or not. Thus the methodology of Strauss becomes more formalized. Its evaluation becomes more a formal one: were the concepts applied correctly? The authors saw this danger and therefore they included the seventh criterion of relevance in their list. They emphasize that a formal application of the procedures of grounded theory building does not necessarily make for 'good research.' Points of reference like the originality of the results from the viewpoint of a potential reader, the relevance of the question, and the relevance of the findings for the fields under study, or even for different fields, play no role here. Another point to reflect on is whether Strauss and Corbin suggest criteria here – which would imply that suggestions were included when a single criterion has been fulfilled or not – or a different form of orientation for assessing a grounded theory study.

In the recent edition of *Basics of Qualitative Research* (Corbin and Strauss, 2015), Corbin takes a different perspective on the quality of grounded theory research. First, she provides a list of features for assessing the quality of qualitative research, not only referring to the grounded theory discourse. Issues are methodological consistency, clarity of purpose of the research, self-awareness, methodological training and awareness, sensitivity to participants and data, for example (2015, pp. 347–9). But then she takes a perspective on the quality of grounded theory studies from the outside, when she provides two lists of checkpoints for researchers and reviewers (pp. 350–2).

The first list of 16 checkpoints ('checkpoints that researchers and reviewers can use to evaluate the methodological consistency of a grounded theory study') address issues like the target sample, the sampling process, alternation of collection and analysis of data, ethical considerations, concepts resulting from theoretical sampling and the data (or the literature), sensitivity to participants and data, description of coding procedures and development of a core category, problems in the research, methodological decisions and adaptions, feedback from peers and participants, and keeping a research journal (pp. 350–1).

The second list of 17 checkpoints ('checkpoints that researchers and reviewers can use to evaluate the quality and applicability of a grounded theory study') address the core category, its relations and coverage, the development of the categories in general, the provision of descriptive data for each category, context, conditions and consequences integrated in the theory, integration of process, explanation of saturation, resonance of the theory with professionals and participants, gaps in the theory, negative cases and variations in the theory, creative presentation of findings, including insights and their significance, potential for pickup in discussions of relevant groups, limitations spelled out, and suggestions for implementation (pp. 351–2). These checkpoints include the essential elements of grounded theory methodology, but do not stick to just checking whether these elements were applied or not. The checkpoints are also a useful orientation for researchers outside the grounded theory field, when they are confronted with papers and proposals referring to grounded theory studies and are expected to evaluate them and take a decision.

Criteria for constructivist grounded theory research

Finally, Charmaz has formulated a set of criteria for evaluating grounded theory research from her constructivist point of view. These include credibility (sufficient data, systematic comparison, enough evidence, and links between data and arguments), originality (fresh categories, new insights, social and theoretical significance, challenge of current ideas), resonance (sense-making for the participants, links to larger collectivities or institutions or individual lives) and usefulness (for peoples' everyday worlds, generic process in the categories, transferability and contribution to making a better world) (see Charmaz, 2014, pp. 337–8). Charmaz does not discuss these criteria in detail, but sees some links between them: 'A strong combination of originality and credibility increases resonance, usefulness and the subsequent value of the contribution' (p. 338). The list she suggests combines process criteria addressing the quality of the study (credibility), relevance criteria (resonance and usefulness) and novelty criteria (originality). Dey (2007, p. 177) discusses notions of validity and validation in this context in a critical way and suggests focusing on theoretical consistency and accuracy of empirical interpretations. For assessing one's efforts in developing or constructing a grounded theory, questions of theoretical saturation should not be restricted to data collection. They should also be applied to the analysis of the data and about the issue under study – was the possible profit from the data taken and also taken from the analysis of the issue? This criterion is not a fixed and formal one but is relative and based on the researcher's judgement and the estimation that relevant additions from continuing the analysis will not come up. In this context, Hood (2007) presents an instructive comparison of grounded theory research with qualitative research in general based on induction from material. From this comparison, she sees three differences as crucial. Research in grounded theory consists of theoretical sampling, constant comparison of data to theoretical categories and a focus on the development of theory via theoretical saturation of categories rather than substantive verifiable findings (p. 163). These differences can be turned into criteria for judging whether a project is really a grounded theory study or if the researchers just claim to have done grounded theory.

CRITERIA FOR EVALUATING THE BUILDING OF THEORIES

In terms of the findings that have already been produced in a particular piece of research, the questions answered through the use of such criteria can be summarized according to Huberman and Miles in aspects such as grounding of findings in data, logical inferences, justification of methodological decisions, researcher bias and credibility (1998, p. 202).

Although the findings are the starting point for evaluating the research, an attempt is made to do this by combining a result-oriented view with a process-oriented view. Such aspects are also included in the criteria suggested by Hammersley (1992, p. 64) in a synopsis of various approaches for evaluating theories developed from empirical field studies (Box 7.2). These criteria are specific to the evaluation of qualitative research and its procedures, methods and results, and they start from theory building as one feature of qualitative research. The procedures that led to the theory – the degree of development of the theory which is the result of this process, and finally the transferability of the theory to other fields and back into the studied context – become central aspects of evaluating all qualitative and grounded theory research.

BOX 7.2 CRITERIA FOR THEORY DEVELOPMENT IN QUALITATIVE RESEARCH

1. The degree to which generic/formal theory is produced.
2. The degree of development of the theory.
3. The novelty of the claims made.
4. The consistency of the claims with empirical observations and the inclusion of representative examples of the latter in the report.
5. The credibility of the account to readers and/or those studied.
6. The extent to which findings are transferable to other settings.
7. The reflexivity of the account: the degree to which the effects on the findings of the researcher and of the research settings employed are assessed and/or the amount of information about the research process that is provided to readers.

(Hammersley, 1992, p. 64)

All in all, the various suggestions made by Glaser, Strauss, Corbin, Charmaz and others show that grounded theory methodologists try to meet requirements for scientific **rigour** by defining criteria for the evaluation of their work. Sometimes, these suggestions are just questions about whether the elements of the research process have been applied or not. Sometimes they provide features that should characterize a theory that came out of the process. Some of the criteria address how the research was done, others are more oriented to the usefulness and relevance of the outcome, which is more a practice-oriented than an academic perspective. The more general question – whether these are really criteria, with a **benchmark** or cut-off point for when they are fulfilled or not and what that means for the evaluation (see Flick, 2018b, for more details) is not discussed in these suggestions.

● KEY POINTS

- Writing is a central part of the research process in grounded theory research.
- This becomes manifest at two points in the process: in memoing and in writing the theory.
- New forms of display such as the conditional matrix and situational maps add to the forms of writing grounded theory.

- In all versions of grounded theory, a number of criteria have been suggested for evaluating grounded theory research and its outcomes.
- In recent versions, issues relevant for reviewers and researchers from outside the field have been considered.

■ FURTHER READING

Issues of writing and assessing in theory development, using grounded theory and, more generally, qualitative research are treated in more detail in the following books:

Charmaz, K. (2014) *Constructing Grounded Theory: A Practical Guide through Qualitative Analysis*. London: Sage.

Flick, U. (2018) *Managing Quality in Qualitative Research* (Book 10 of *The SAGE Qualitative Research Kit*, 2nd ed.). London: Sage.

Gibbs, G.R. (2018) *Analyzing Qualitative Data* (Book 6 of *The SAGE Qualitative Research Kit*, 2nd ed.). London: Sage.

CHAPTER EIGHT

ADVANCING
RESEARCH DESIGN IN GROUNDED THEORY

CONTENTS

CHAPTER OBJECTIVES

After reading this chapter, you should know about:

- the contribution that a stronger recognition of designing research could make to doing grounded theory research;
- how research designs can help to make grounded theory research less tied to the researchers' intuition;
- the basic designs that could be used in grounded theory; and
- the components of research designs that are relevant in grounded theory research.

INTRODUCTION

In the preceding chapters, an outline of the various versions of grounded theory research that are currently existing side by side or in competition has been given. If we regard these versions as the state of the art in grounded theory methodology, from the perspective of doing grounded theory and in particular from that of some-one trying to start doing research with a grounded theory project, some of the major orientations may seem a bit vague and to ask for a lot of intuition from the research-ers (see below). In this and the following chapters, we will try to offer concepts for getting out of this intuition trap. In this chapter we will concentrate on how to design research, an issue that is largely absent in the grounded theory literature. *The SAGE Handbook of Grounded Theory* (Bryant and Charmaz, 2007b) and the textbooks by Charmaz (2014), Holton and Walsh (2017), Bryant (2017) and others demon-strate this absence. Thinking about research designs has been long associated with controlling bias in quantitative research. Therefore, it is neither that widespread in qualitative research in general nor very much part of the grounded theory vocabu-lary. However, if we understand this term in a less narrow way, it may be helpful for addressing issues that have always been relevant for grounded theory research and still are. The use of the ideas in the background of this wider concept of research design has been more or less implicit in grounded theory practice without explicitly using or discussing the term as a principle. An example is the notion of Becker et al. (1961) that a research design in studies similar to what was later called 'grounded theory' emerges in the end rather than in the beginning of a study. In this chapter, the idea of a qualitative research design will be discussed in relation to its contribu-tion to spelling out the planning and doing of research in grounded theory more explicitly. How far it can make explicit and transparent what is done in (successful) grounded theory research, often implicitly, will be discussed.

Vague intuitionalism in grounded theory methodology

The aim of this chapter is to make the term 'research design' more explicit in its relevance for grounded theory. The starting point for this is the impression that methodological discussions in grounded theory sometimes have been based since their beginning on some kind of *vague intuitionalism*. This makes it a bit difficult to transfer these discussions into future use – to teaching grounded theory to novices and to planning and conducting new projects. This vague intuitionalism includes: (1) the claim of intuition in the field, which makes the research work ('just do it!' – Glaser, 1992); and (2) the uniqueness of the founding fathers as researchers, personalities and teachers which is difficult to replicate in new research or learning. This vague intuitionalism also includes (3) the idea of flexibility in the field – to develop and choose methodological approaches, kinds of data and cases in the process (according to the idea of emergent methods) and finish when saturation has been reached. These principles are challenging when they are to be applied in new research with novices to qualitative research or grounded theory. This vague intuitionalism finally includes (4) the emphasis on abduction as the principle of inference and reasoning; and (5) the idea of discovering theories in the field. Again, these ideas should be recognized as important but they are also difficult to transfer to new research(ers). We will begin with the last two aspects, which in recent developments have in some ways increased this vague intuitionalism.

Abduction as a principle of discovery in grounded theory research

The idea of abduction has become quite prominent in the recent grounded theory discourse as a main principle of reasoning (Reichertz, 2007; Charmaz, 2014; Thornberg and Charmaz, 2014; Kennedy and Thornberg, 2018; see Chapters 1, 5 and 6). Abduction was originally introduced by the pragmatist Charles Sanders Peirce (1878/1958) as a third principle of reasoning in addition to induction and deduction. Given the debates in grounded theory between the Glaserian approach (which strongly emphasizes a more or less pure inductivism as a feature of grounded theory; see Chapters 1 and 4) and the Strauss and Corbin approach (suggesting a combination of induction and deduction once their second step of axial coding has been reached – see Kelle, 2005; and again Chapters 1 and 4), the appeal of abduction may also be to show a way out of this debate. However, the price for this way out is the stronger emphasis on creativity and intuition in proceeding along this path of inquiry. We cannot go deeper into this debate here (see Chapter 1), but for the issue of vague intuitionalism it is relevant to see that younger researchers doing a PhD often lack the expertise of Glaser, Strauss, Charmaz or Bryant, and are left alone to make creativity, abduction and discovery work in their research.

Constructing grounded theories

A second turn led from seeing grounded theory research as a process of intuitive discovery by using methods, to understanding it as a process of constructing theories and taking specific decisions regarding methods and fields, and regarding selecting people, events and materials as data (see Charmaz, 2014). This is a major step towards 'grounding' the research in grounded theory in the researchers' activities and choices in the field (see Chapter 5).

From sacred data to unearthing hidden meanings

In the development of grounded theory as a field, the original understanding of the concept of data has been challenged. Statements such as 'All is data' (Glaser, 2002) highlight this original understanding. Glaser and Strauss (1967) already had a rather pragmatic approach to the concept of data, when they stated 'that what is required are some imagination, some ingenuity and, most of all, a considerable shift in attitude toward qualitative materials themselves' (1967, p. 161). As we saw in Chapter 3, Clarke (2005) is rather sceptical about the idea of 'letting data speak for themselves' and 'awaiting emergence' from the data (pp. 75–6). Clarke thus takes up an essential aspect of the intuitionalism mentioned above. In the original versions of grounded theory research, theoretical insights in general and categories in a technical sense 'emerge' from the data if the researchers are only open enough in the field (and not 'disoriented' by taking existing theories into account). In her considerations, Clarke makes a point of going beyond this basic concept of grounded theory – a (more or less experienced) researcher turns to an interesting field in a very open manner and discovers what is going on there by letting the data and categories emerge. Clarke emphasizes that once research starts less from such a general interest or curiosity but from an existing inequality (as in feminist or social-problems-oriented research), you should invest more in planning the research and in systematizing the data collection. This brings us to the concept that is the main topic of this chapter.

Stages of expertise

The wider background for the following considerations is based on the (interrelated) five-stage models of (developing) expertise in the areas of nursing (Benner, 1982) and of artificial intelligence (Dreyfus and Dreyfus, 1986). These stages range from *novice* (stage 1) through *advanced beginner* (2), *competent* (3), *proficient* (4) and *expert* (5). It would go beyond the scope of this chapter to discuss these models and their stages in detail. The interesting point in our context is that the first stages of expertise are strongly based on rules that are applied to concrete situations and explicit knowledge. Only the fifth stage (expert) is more and more based on intuition and tacit knowledge and operates without reference to rules and explicit knowledge. Applied to our context, much of the methodological literature on how to do grounded theory starts from examples of expertise that work with intuition and tacit knowledge and less with explication of rules, steps and methods.

DESIGNING GROUNDED THEORY RESEARCH

What is linked to the term 'research design' in social research? In the next section, several understandings of this term will be discussed in a comparative way. In quantitative research, 'research design' is strongly linked to controlling and standardization of research situations to increase or assure the validity and reliability of the research and its outcomes, which are both not objectives of grounded theory (research). Beyond these aspects of standardization and control, designing a study includes a wider range of aspects. A more general definition comes from Charles Ragin, who sees a research design as 'a plan for collecting and analyzing evidence that will make it possible for the investigator to answer whatever questions he or she has posed' (1994, p. 191). This concept refers to all aspects of the research process.

DESIGN IN THE PROCESS

That an interest in research design is not very prominent in grounded theory may have several reasons. A first reason may be the current understanding of grounded theory as an emergent method as outlined by Charmaz (2008, p. 155) as inductive, indeterminate and open-ended. In the general discussion about emergent methods (see Hesse-Biber and Leavy, 2008), ideas of planning a project by outlining a research design are also not very prominent (although exceptions such as Wright, 2009, exist). In linking the discourses of grounded theory and emergent methods, the role of emergence in grounded theory research becomes a double one: not only are the 'findings' of grounded theory research (i.e. the categories developed and used and also the resulting theory) understood as emerging (in particular in classic grounded theory, see Glaser, 1992; Holton and Walsh, 2017; and critically Kelle, 2014), but also the use of methods. This may be a good perspective for retrospectively describing the process and use of methodological tools in a successful study by expert research- ers. However, the question here is again, whether this is a helpful orientation for a grounded theory study still to be undertaken and for novices in the field.

Second, that the interest in research design has not played a big role in the grounded theory vocabulary can be traced back to the very early studies and maybe finds its reasons in them. Becker et al. (1961) show in some sense a quite typical understanding of the term 'research design' in grounded theory. Although the book about their study (*Boys in White*) has a chapter on 'research design', they begin it with the statement: 'In one sense, our study had no design' (1961, p. 17). But then they show how their design developed in the process of their research, which became more and more systematic and consistent along the way.

In a similar way, Hammersley and Atkinson (1995, p. 24) argue in the context of ethnography that 'research design should be a reflexive process which operates throughout every stage of a project'. Such a flexible understanding of the term 'research design' opens a perspective for using it in the context of grounded theory as an emergent method (Charmaz, 2008).

Thus we may state at this point that there seems to be (at least in comparison to quantitative research) a less concrete concept of designing research in qualitative and grounded theory research. However, we can outline the focus of this concept. First of all, a research design here is not something set up at one point of the preparation of a project and then just applied in the field. It rather is developed (or emerging) in the process of the project and in the conditions of the field that is studied. It has more to do with the researchers reflecting the research and field in this process and less with defining the design at the desk of the methodologist beforehand. Second, research design refers to more than validity issues.

Approaches to research designs referring to grounded theory

'Research design' is used in a different way when referring to grounded theory research. Creswell (2013) discusses five major approaches (or traditions) of qualitative research – among them grounded theory. He then describes the characteristics of the approaches and sees doing research according to these characteristics as selecting a research design (such as grounded theory, for example), which he sees as a qualitative research design (Creswell, 2013, p. 83). Taking up such an approach is then the main aspect of designing qualitative research. How far this understanding – grounded theory as one major research design in qualitative research – takes into account that there are now several versions of how to understand and do grounded theory, remains open. Creswell refers both to Corbin and Strauss (2008) and Charmaz (2014) when describing the procedures of doing grounded theory. At the same time, the more concrete issues of how to use grounded theory in a concrete field and the decisions to be taken in this process and project remain secondary, in Creswell's treatment. At least this concept of research design forces researchers to reflect and account for why they selected grounded theory as the approach for their study. Creswell's arguments about research design (in 2014) in general continuously move between designing how to do the study (in the above sense) and designing writings about it (proposals at the beginning or reports at the end).

In her reflections about the need for stronger planning of grounded theory, Clarke (2005, p. 77) points out that the issue of research design leads right away to the contested areas in the disputes between Strauss and Glaser. She also discusses their differing approaches and her own (situational analysis) as some kind of **basic design** in grounded theory without going into details. However, she outlines her view on research design: 'that we also need to *design* our research from the outset in order to explicitly gather data about theoretically and substantively underdeveloped areas that may lie in our situations of inquiry' (Clarke, 2005, p. 76).

COMPONENTS OF RESEARCH DESIGNS AND THEIR RELEVANCE FOR GROUNDED THEORY RESEARCH

In other cases, research design is described as including several components. Maxwell (2013, p. 5) sees purposes, conceptual context, methods and validity as such components grouped around the central one (the research question). In his 'interactive model of research design', the term design itself is not visible (see Figure 8.1).

This again has a process approach to designing qualitative research in general and includes some kind of interaction or negotiation between the components

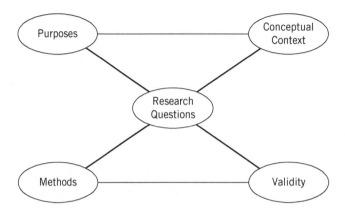

FIGURE 8.1 An interactive model of research design

Source: Maxwell, 2013, p. 5

that are included. This understanding of design is open to adapting the research to the conditions in the field and of the issue that is studied and thus comes closer to grounded theory research – even when understood as an emerging method – than other concepts of research design. Maxwell sees aspects such as purposes of a study, the conceptual context, methods, validity and research questions as interdependent. Seeing these components in an interactive model, this concept allows changes in the methods used in the field, and the (further) development of the conceptual context, as in a grounded theory study. Maxwell's model is also based on rejecting the dominance of any one of its components (e.g. the research question), which is often supposed to define the other components mentioned in the model. Bryman (2007) has studied empirically how researchers deal with the issue of research questions. He makes a distinction between a *universalistic* model and a *particularistic* model. In the particularistic model, the research question has a particular role for designing the research in detail, which includes that the question drives the decision for a specific approach or research programme (e.g. for taking a grounded theory approach). In the universalistic model, the dominance of the research question becomes relative to the adherence to a specific understanding of research – researchers who have always used grounded theory will tend to use it also in a new study and adapt the research question so that this approach will work. However, it can be discussed whether the components in Maxwell's model are the only ones relevant in designing qualitative research in a concrete way. This question becomes even more important if we take grounded theory as a point of reference.

In my own works about qualitative research designs (see Flick, 2018c), I discuss several components of research design in a qualitative study, which can be summarized in four major areas:

a. The *aims of the study* include its *general goals* and its *generalization goals*: what is the intention behind doing the study? In our context a major aim can be to develop a theory about a specific phenomenon in the field under study or to provide detailed descriptions of the field and phenomenon. Other aims can be the evaluation of a process or service. Generalization goals can on the one hand refer to making statements about the phenomenon in the field (or case) that was studied or more general statements beyond it. In the case of grounded theory this distinction is taken up in the difference between substantive theories (referring to a phenomenon in a field) and formal theory (referring to a phenomenon in several fields). For Glaser (2002), such a generalization seems to be a major goal; for constructivist grounded theorists, it may be a product of their research, but being attentive to positionality precedes generalizing. Thus generalizations can be a major part of an understanding of grounded theory as an emergent method (Charmaz, 2008).

b. *Aspects brought to the field* include the *theoretical framework* and the concrete *research questions* to be answered. The theoretical framework can become concrete in the sensitizing concepts that are used for disclosing a field or phenomenon under study. It can also refer to several levels, such as theories about the issue under study and the more methodological assumptions of the research programme that is pursued. The first aspect may be surprising in the context of grounded theory research where the theories are supposed to be discovered in the field. But as the recent discussions about the use of the literature in grounded theory research (see Dunne, 2011; and Chapter 1) demonstrate, existing theoretical and empirical knowledge plays an increasingly important role in grounded theory research as well, if only as a challenge to be dealt with. The second level in the theoretical framework (i.e. the methodological assumptions of the research programme used as orientation) is becoming more and more relevant the more the field of grounded theory research proliferates – in Glaser's approach, Strauss and Corbin's approach, Charmaz's approach and Clarke's approach. This is further proliferated by the versions of grounded theory research developed in nursing (see Morse et al., 2009) and in management research (see Fendt and Sachs, 2008), for example. The version and its understanding of research and of grounded theory practices will influence what the researcher adopting it will do in the concrete study and field and thus influence the design of the study.

c. *Methods and methodology* includes three aspects: the *selection of empirical material*, the *methodological procedures* that are applied, and the *degree of standardization and control* in the way the research is done. In the first aspect, the differentiation of Morse (2007) shows that grounded theory research is not necessarily limited to theoretical sampling, but that before it other forms of sampling are applied. Which forms of selecting cases, materials and so on are used has a strong influence on the design of the concrete study. The methodological procedures on the one hand include strategies of data collection or, in the case of naturally occurring data (see Toerien, 2014; Potter and Shaw, 2018; and Chapter 3), the use of existing data (photos, recordings, documents). Which of these to use should be decided according to which phenomenon and field is to be studied. On the other hand, the methodological procedures include the ways these data are analyzed. Here again, the term 'using grounded theory coding' has proliferated according to the versions of grounded theory mentioned above. Which one is selected and applied (or taken as an orientation) is a major decision in constructing a research design in grounded theory research. The third aspect, standardization and control, mostly plays a minor role in the openness characterizing methodological approaches in grounded theory. However, once research teams work in a project and develop some degree of sharing the work, a consensus about how to proceed in the field and with the data seems necessary (see Cornish et al., 2014) also in a grounded theory project.

d. *Practical framework conditions* of doing a study include the *temporal, personal, and material resources* that are available. These aspects are often underestimated in planning a study; they not only refer to financial resources that can be used or the timescale of a project (e.g. in the context of a thesis) but also the research experience and skills of the researchers that are involved. Although grounded theory often is seen as easy to do (as it does not seem to involve highly developed methodological skills, for example), resources become a factor in design, at the latest when the research proves to be more complicated than expected. Enough experience in the field and with research seems important for taking the right decisions in sampling, analyzing the data – and stopping the research.

BASIC DESIGNS IN QUALITATIVE RESEARCH AND THEIR RELEVANCE FOR GROUNDED THEORY RESEARCH

Earlier in the chapter we have discussed the idea of equating research designs with approaches, as in the case of the distinctions Creswell (2013) has suggested. This idea might not contribute much to using the concept of research design for improving or advancing grounded theory research, as it basically sees the latter as a research design. As we saw in the preceding section, there are many design issues inside a grounded theory approach, which are neglected if grounded theory itself is declared a design. In what follows a different perspective is taken, when we discuss the basic designs identified elsewhere (see Flick, 2018c) for their relevance for grounded theory research (see Figure 8.2).

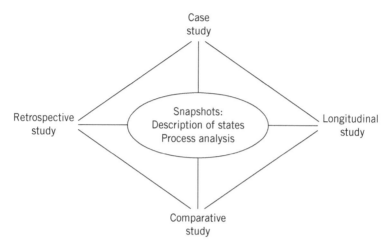

FIGURE 8.2   Basic designs in qualitative research

Source: Flick, 2014, p. 130

For a more systematic approach to these basic research designs we can take two perspectives: one (a) focusing on the dimension of comparison, and the other (b) on the dimension of development and process over time.

a.   Comparison is a major principle and feature of grounded theory research as Glaser and Strauss (1967) and in particular Glaser (1969) already have clarified in the principle of the constant comparative method outlined in Chapter 4. *Comparison* as an organizing principle in designing qualitative research covers two main alternatives: *case studies* and *comparative studies*. Again the difference lies in the degree of explicitness. A comparative study in most examples is defined by a number of cases (e.g. people, institutions, settings, etc.) that are in the focus of the research right away. Often these cases are not analyzed in a holistic manner, but one or several dimensions of comparison are defined. These dimensions can be relevant in selecting the cases, in juxtaposing elements or excerpts and the like. Defining these dimensions right away makes the comparison in the project explicit and the project a comparative study. For grounded theory research, such a comparative study of several cases can be a starting point for developing first concepts based on the expected differences between the cases. A case study takes a more holistic approach to the single case (field, institution, person, setting). Of course, a case study includes comparison as well – between members of an institution, between incidents in the field, for example. Dimensions of such comparison may develop along the way. That is why comparison is more implicit here if seen from a research design angle. It is also implicit because the selection of the single case is often the result of an implicit comparison with other possible cases, which then defines why this case and no other one is studied. For a grounded theory study, this implicit comparison becomes relevant in selecting the field to study, in developing the constant comparison and in selecting the next case(s) to continue with. A case study design can also comprise a series of cases that are studied one after the other. (Suggestions for how to complement grounded theory coding for analyzing cases such as interviewees are made in Chapter 5.)

b. *Time and process* is another essential in grounded theory research, as studies such as Corbin and Strauss (1988) may demonstrate. As a design principle in qualitative research and grounded theory, we can distinguish three basic research designs along this dimension – snapshots; **longitudinal studies** and retrospective research. The first design focuses on a given state at a specific moment – what is the way of dealing with the knowledge about someone dying in a specific period, perhaps in several settings, and what kind of grounded theory can be developed from empirical research? The second adopts the idea of longitudinal research – and to focus the empirical research and theory development on process and change over time by collecting data repeatedly and comparing the several field contacts and data. The third basic research design is more often used in qualitative research to cover process and development. Here the approach is retrospective – for example, by using biographical or narrative data for reconstructing the process that led to a current state. In our example, the focus here would be about the changes in dealing with death, or the dying of a person (e.g. knowledge and communication about this over the last 20 years). These basic designs can in some ways be combined, in a retrospective case study or a longitudinal comparative study, for instance. They can also be triangulated – for example, a snapshot (e.g. observations in the here and now of the participants' practices) can be complemented by a more retrospective approach (e.g. the participants' migration histories).

CONCLUSION

The suggestions for how to design qualitative research made so far can be used to make what is done in grounded theory research a bit more systematic. Without going into further details or suggestions, this need is also stated in general by Clarke (2005,

p. 76). Spelling out design issues in grounded theory will not only make the research more systematic but make it easier to plan new projects and to teach the approach to novices in the beginning, and with intuitionalism emphasized less as a basic principle. Whether this systematization can be advanced by a more explicit use of triangulation in grounded theory will be discussed in the next chapter.

● KEY POINTS

- Concepts of grounded theory come with a strong demand for the researchers' intuition.
- To think about grounded theory in terms of designing research may contribute to making the research easier to plan.
- This applies mainly to novice researchers.
- Components of designs can support this kind of rationality in the research.
- Basic designs give an orientation.

■ FURTHER READING

The following texts address the issues of this chapter implicitly for grounded theory or in more detail for qualitative research in general:

Charmaz, K. (2014) *Constructing Grounded Theory – A Practical Guide through Qualitative Analysis*, 2nd ed. Thousand Oaks, CA: Sage.

Clarke, A. (2005) *Situational Analysis: Grounded Theory after the Postmodern Turn.* Thousand Oaks, CA: Sage.

Flick, U. (2014) *An Introduction to Qualitative Research*, 5th ed. London: Sage.

Flick, U. (2018) *Designing Qualitative Research* (Book 1 of *The SAGE Qualitative Research Kit*, 2nd ed.). London: Sage.

CHAPTER NINE

BECOMING SYSTEMATIC
TRIANGULATION IN GROUNDED THEORY

CHAPTER OBJECTIVES

After reading this chapter, you should know:

- the background of triangulation;
- how triangulation was used implicitly in grounded theory research; and
- which forms of triangulation could be used in grounded theory research.

TRIANGULATION IN GROUNDED THEORY

In the preceding chapter, we discussed the concept of research design as a way of advancing grounded theory research and of making it more easily usable by new researchers in general or those using grounded theory in the field. The idea behind that chapter was that the concept 'research design' had not been used so much in grounded theory discourses but that some of the issues linked to it played a role implicitly. Using these ideas and the concept more explicitly could both advance and facilitate grounded theory research. In this chapter we will take a similar perspective on the concept of triangulation and its possible relevance for grounded theory research. *The SAGE Handbook of Grounded Theory* (Bryant and Charmaz, 2007b) and textbooks by Charmaz (2014), Holton and Walsh (2017) and Bryant (2017) again show that triangulation is also not very prominent as a concept in grounded theory methodology discussions. However, the ideas behind triangulation are not too far away from what is done in grounded theory research. The main idea of triangulation is to extend the research by using several methods, differing theories or multiple researchers. The resulting extension of data and interpretations in the process is seen as a contribution to making research and results more credible and fruitful. 'Triangulation' has long been (mis-)understood as simple confirmation of results with other results or with results from using other methods to study the same phenomenon. Again this may look like something that is not very relevant as a principle for methodological discussions in grounded theory. One example of an implicit use of these ideas is the early statement of Glaser and Strauss (1967) that grounded theory research should work with various 'slices of data'. This is similar to the concept of 'data triangulation' (Denzin, 1970; Flick, 2018a) without spelling it out in a methodological way (see below).

Background of the concept

Triangulation has a long history in the social sciences (see Flick, 2018a), but in qualitative research it became prominent with Denzin's suggestions (1970), in which he distinguished four forms: ***Data* triangulation** combines various sorts of data (e.g. interviews and observations). ***Investigator* triangulation** includes several researchers and their perspectives on the issue. ***Theoretical* triangulation** uses various theoretical approaches and combines them. Most prominent is *methodological* triangulation focusing on combining several methodological approaches in one method (***within-method* triangulation**) or in several independent methods (***between-methods* triangulation**). In the beginning the use of triangulation was oriented toward confirming results from one method with those coming from a second approach, but the discussion has since developed further.

Development of the concept

We can distinguish several phases in the development of the concept (see Flick, 2018e): 'triangulation 1.0' characterizes the original concept suggested by Denzin (1970), aiming at validation by playing off methods against each other. This version was heavily criticized in the following years (for an overview, see Flick, 1992), but still is the one referred to in discussions about mixed methods (e.g. in Mark, 2015; or Creswell, 2014, p. 201). In his later publications (e.g. Denzin, 1989, p. 246) and in responding to the critiques mentioned above, Denzin sees triangulation in a more differentiated way and as a strategy on the road to a deeper understanding of an issue under study, and thus as a step toward more knowledge and less toward validity and objectivity in interpretation. In this version, triangulation is also no longer understood as a strategy for confirming findings from one approach by findings from using another approach. Rather, triangulation is aiming at broader, deeper, more comprehensive understandings of what is studied, and that often includes – or heads toward – discrepancies and contradictions in the findings. Denzin uses the term 'triangulation 2.0' (Denzin, 2012) to highlight this shift in the concept. It is also relevant in his distinction of triangulation from mixed methods. Further developing this reformulation of triangulation includes a number of suggestions for spelling out the concept in a more differentiated way (Flick, 2018e). In a *weak programme* of triangulation, the focus is on confirming results (as mentioned above), on using it as a criterion for assessing the quality of qualitative research (as in Lincoln and Guba's, 1985, criterion of credibility, which builds upon triangulation) and on a rather pragmatic combination of methods. In a *strong programme* of triangulation, the focus is on collecting new insights rather than confirming the ones already obtained. Triangulation then is more a strategy towards extra knowledge and is an extension of a research programme, which includes the systematic selection of various methods and the combination of research perspectives linked to these methods. In such a combination, a systematic triangulation of perspectives (see Flick, 1992) should be included – different forms of knowledge, or knowledge and practices, or experiences from various actors in the field. Finally, this strong programme of triangulation comprises the idea of a ***comprehensive* triangulation**: Denzin (1970) had seen data and investigator, theoretical and methodological triangulation as alternatives, of which researchers should select one. In a comprehensive triangulation, several investigators collaborate (investigator triangulation) and bring their different theoretical perspectives (disciplinary backgrounds for example – theoretical triangulation) to the research. This may lead to the combination of several methods (methodological triangulation), which provide several forms of data to be combined (data collection). To summarize these more recent developments, the term 'triangulation 3.0' (see Flick, 2018e) is used.

THE RELEVANCE OF TRIANGULATION FOR GROUNDED THEORY
Data triangulation: slices of data

As there are only a few explicit references linking triangulation and grounded theory, we will explain this connection a bit more using both implicit and explicit links between both. If we go back to Glaser and Strauss (1967), we find their ideas about using 'slices of data' (p. 65) in the context of theoretical sampling 'which give the analyst different views or vantage points from which to understand a category and to develop its properties'. This idea comes very close to what Denzin later (1970) developed as 'data triangulation'; in particular, when the latter is not used for validating but for extending the knowledge that is developed. Glaser and Strauss see the multiplicity of perspectives as an aim of collecting the slices of data. The differences in perspective will not lead to relativism, if they are subjected to a comparative analysis, but will make the developed theory more comprehensive (1967, p. 68).

If we turn these suggestions into some kind of advice for planning future research projects using grounded theory, the suggestion is to plan systematically the use of several kinds of data, to pursue their production systematically to be able to compare them for their differences and commonalities. For example, in our study about homeless adolescents and chronic illness, we interviewed adolescents about their perceptions of their diseases, of their symptoms and about their experiences with seeking and using professional treatment. At the same time, we interviewed people working with this target group or who could be approached by the adolescents in case of problems (service providers). We asked them about their perceptions of homeless adolescents and about what they saw as reasons why the adolescents turned to professional help or did not. All in all, it became obvious that the perceptions of the adolescents and of the service providers about dealing with chronic illness on the street were in some respects only slightly different, and in other respects completely different. The latter was the case for the evaluation of the relevance of alcohol and drugs as a problem solver (as seen by the adolescents) or as a problem intensifier (as seen by the service providers). At the same time the adolescents and service providers differed in their perceptions of health-related need for help. The adolescents saw a rather limited need for such help, the physicians and social workers saw a very strong need (see Flick, 2011). This approach should allow us to take diverse perspectives on the issue and field under study and to triangulate them in a systematic way.

Investigator triangulation: diversity in teamwork composition

Qualitative research in general is often based on collaborative teamwork (see Cornish et al., 2014). In particular, in the writings of Strauss (1987) and Glaser and Strauss (1967) the role of teamwork in grounded theory becomes clear. In Box 9.1, this practice is illustrated from the work of Strauss et al. (1964).

BOX 9.1   INVESTIGATOR TRIANGULATION IN GROUNDED THEORY

There were three fieldworkers subjected for the most part to the same raw data. Search for pinpointing and negative evidence was abetted by the collective nature of our inquiry. If the colleague reported the same kind of observation as another without prior consultation, confidence grew. If after hearing the report of an observation, a colleague was himself able unquestionably to duplicate it, it indicated that our observational techniques had some degree of reliability. If no colleague did corroborate an observation – which did happen – if it seemed important then, or later, further inquiry was initiated. Something like a built-in reliability check was thus obtained because several fieldworkers were exposed directly to similar or identical data.

(Strauss et al., 1964, p. 36)

Wiener (2007) has described this collaboration in more detail for the example of a research project led by Strauss. She emphasizes the diversity in the team members' backgrounds – theoretically, professionally, in their interests and in their experience with the issue under study (2007, pp. 294, 297). However, this account of the research emphasizes that the people involved had these diverse backgrounds and how fruitful this was, and the outcome of this process was very much 'grounded' in the personality of the project's leader and how he managed the process. For planning further grounded theory projects, the idea of systematically integrating researchers with different (methodological or theoretical) backgrounds into a research team can be seen as an application of investigator triangulation.

Theoretical triangulation as confrontation of research perspectives

Theoretical triangulation usually refers to combining (or juxtaposing) several substantial theories. In the context of grounded theory, theoretical triangulation refers to combining the approach of grounded theory with other research approaches or perspectives. This could refer to actual research or methodological programmes – such as combining grounded theory and discourse analysis (as in Clarke, 2005), but it also refers to taking a theoretical perspective into the analysis of data in a grounded theory study. So we find a number of examples in which a grounded theory approach has been triangulated with a different theoretical research perspective. Rennie (2000) has developed triangulation into a more integrative approach, seeing grounded theory as 'methodical hermeneutics'. The methodologically relevant question, however, is what the function of this different theoretical perspective for a grounded theory is. Wilson and Hutchinson (1991), for example, have triangulated Heideggerian hermeneutics and grounded theory as two 'qualitative methods'.

This means that the one approach – hermeneutics – is seen as the perspective that provides the insights (into meanings and practices), and grounded theory is located around the implementation of these insights into further research and interventions. Annells (2006) has taken this article as a starting point for developing the triangulation of Heideggerian hermeneutics and grounded theory into using them in two distinct phases of a research project (2006, p. 58). Here, the role of both approaches is seen on a comparable level; both are complementary in producing insights. Kushner and Morrow (2003) have used the term 'theoretical triangulation' for bringing together grounded, feminist and critical theory: 'We propose a third path that focuses on the interplay between grounded, feminist, and critical theories, as a strategy that provides a more comprehensive account of the relations between agency, structure, and critique' (2003, p. 30). Their understanding of theoretical triangulation means a 'constant grounding process at the level of data gathering and analysis, coupled with internal checks (constant comparisons in the terminology of grounded theory) on theoretical arguments based on back and forth movement between questions posed with both feminist and critical theories' (2003, p. 38). In this example the question arises of how far the feminist and critical theories delimit what can be developed from empirical material into a grounded theory. Gibson (2007, p. 443) criticizes this suggestion by Kushner and Morrow (2003) as rather unclear in the details of what the authors suggest doing and what the meaning of this is. However, this could be another example of taking other (theoretical) approaches into account for advancing the process of grounded theory development in the tradition of (theoretical) triangulation.

In their book Wertz et al. (2011) provide the results of a more practical triangulation of several theoretical approaches with grounded theory used in the step of analyzing empirical material. The authors take one interview and analyze it using five different research perspectives (among them grounded theory, discourse analysis and narrative research). The book also provides some detailed comparison of pairs of approaches, produced as differences and similarities in analyzing the text. It also becomes evident that not only the procedure of how the text is analyzed, but also which aspects are put in the foreground varies across the five approaches. Thus we find 'constructing a grounded theory of loss and regaining a valued self' (Charmaz, 2011) as the approach and result of the grounded theory method. The discourse analysis of the same material focuses on 'enhancing oneself, diminishing others' (McMullen, 2011). Thus this book provides an interesting insight into the differences and commonalities of various theoretical perspectives behind the empirical approaches to the same material.

Methodological triangulation between and within methods in grounded theory research

For research practice in the context of grounded theory research, methodological triangulation may be the most relevant aspect. Here we can, similar to in ethnography, distinguish between implicit triangulation (see Flick, 2018a, Chapter 4, for this) and an explicit use of the concept. In implicit triangulation, several methods and data are used and combined in an ad-hoc manner, and sometimes the methods are applied less systematically than flexibly reacting to the challenges and opportunities from the field. In a more explicit triangulation, ethnography as an approach focusing on observations may be combined with, for example, a specific interview method, which is applied in a more systematic way (see Flick, 2018a). Or, alternatively, within an ethnography, several methods (such as observation and interviewing) are triangulated in a systematic way again – a specific form of interviewing is part of the overall design and combined with observation and document analysis, and are both applied systematically again. This distinction can be transferred to grounded theory research. Either several approaches are combined in a grounded theory study in an ad-hoc manner and thus the triangulation remains implicit. Or a grounded theory approach is triangulated with other methodological approaches or several methods are triangulated in a grounded theory study in a more systematic way. Both can be understood as explicit triangulation. In Denzin's (1970) terminology, these forms of combinations are called 'between methods' triangulation.

Within-method triangulation refers to combining several approaches in one method. If grounded theory is understood as a *method*, this could again include several strategies of collecting data (observation, talking to people, analyzing documents, etc.), but it can be discussed whether it is helpful to see this approach as a method.

An example may illustrate the idea of within-method triangulation in a bit more detail. The idea is that several methodological approaches with differing backgrounds are combined in one method to access a phenomenon in a more comprehensive way. The episodic interview (see Flick, 2000, 2018a; and Chapter 3) starts from the notion that people have various forms of knowledge about an issue. These forms should be addressed in different ways. Episodic knowledge refers to concrete situations in which certain experiences have been made ('My first day in school …'). Semantic knowledge refers to more general concepts ('A good teacher is …'). The first form of knowledge can be accessed best in narratives, when asking interviewees to recount specific situations ('Could you please remember your first experience with school and tell me about this situation?'). The second form can be accessed by asking questions ('What is a good teacher for you?'). The combination of both forms of data (small-scale narratives with statements such as definitions, etc.) can give a broader understanding of the issue under study, in particular if it is a phenomenon we do not know much about. This will make such a form of interviewing more relevant for grounded theory research than other forms. This form of interview, which is based on within-method triangulation, can be integrated into a research design based on between-methods triangulation.

AN EXAMPLE OF USING TRIANGULATION: MIGRATION AND LONG-TERM UNEMPLOYMENT

In a recent study (see Flick et al., 2017), the focus of research was on understanding the experiences and problems of migrants to Germany from the former Soviet Union and Turkey with being long-term unemployed and with the institutions that were supposed to help them find work again (called 'job centres') and provide basic social support. The latter was linked to the condition that the recipients were actively seeking regular employment. The design of this research was a comparative study, one linking a retrospective approach with a snapshot. Several methods were triangulated – episodic interviews (see also Chapter 3) and 'go-alongs' (Kusenbach, 2018) with the migrants complemented by focus groups with them and **expert interview**s with job centre staff. The intention behind using these methods was to take different perspectives on the phenomenon of migrant long-term unemployment.

The episodic interviews in this study addressed both episodic knowledge (referring to concrete situations and circumstance – e.g. when I first lost my job ...) and semantic knowledge (referring to concepts and connections between them – e.g., what does work mean to them? What is the relevance of unemployment?). In technical terms the episodic interview aimed at combining small-scale situation narratives with question–answer sequences. Interviewees were invited to recount situations relevant to them in the context of the study's topic – e.g. about how they came to Germany, how they tried and found access (or failed) to regular work, to professional support or experiences with job centres and service providers, or how they developed or maintained social networks in their 'new' environment. Questions beyond that invitation to recount situations and experiences referred to the interviewees' representations of work or of unemployment, for example. Main areas covered in the interviews were work- and/or unemployment-related experiences and practices; help-seeking behaviour experiences with the social support system and expectations about help. The interviews were conducted in German or consecutively interpreted or completely done and transcribed in Russian (or Turkish) and then verbatim translated to German. To extend our understanding of how our participants lived with being unemployed and their experiences of support and control by the institutions we used 'go-alongs' (Kusenbach, 2018) as a second methodological approach. This method aims at gaining insights into the local life worlds of the study participants, getting closer to their own everyday relevancies and being able to analyze socio-spatial integration. Participants were asked to suggest the spatial centres of their everyday life as meeting points, from which places of major importance for them should be accessible within walking distance. Then participants were asked to describe spots of great importance to them – places they liked, disliked or just used regularly – with the help of a street map and then walked with us to some of these places. The choice of the places shown and the route taken was left to the participants. While walking around they explained particular meanings and talked about activities associated with these places. This approach goes beyond regular interviews in two respects. First, the go-along takes the research into the localized life worlds of our participants. This allows us to analyze perceptions of participants' everyday spaces. Second, it allows us to analyze life worlds and spaces from the participants' perspectives and to complement these perspectives with the researchers' perspectives. In this sense, the methodological approaches allow a systematic triangulation of perspectives. Data were analyzed by using thematic coding (see Chapter 4) and the study can be seen as a first step in the longer process of constructing a grounded theory of the phenomenon under study.

CONCLUSION

As we saw earlier in this and the preceding chapters, grounded theory studies often rely on a rather intuitionalist approach, in which they end up in having developed some kind of research design along the way. At the same time, using several methods, combining data, or having several investigators is often part of doing the study. If we take models of expertise as a background (see Chapter 8) for transferring the skills of doing grounded theory to novices, it will be helpful to spell out these implicit practices of triangulating in grounded theory in a more explicit way. This will then allow us to use the potential of triangulation in grounded theory to apply a systematic triangulation of perspectives (of several actors in the field, for example) to the issue under study.

● KEY POINTS

- Triangulation can contribute to making the use of methods and perspectives in a grounded theory study more explicit.
- There are a number of approaches that implicitly use triangulation in grounded theory, but the systematic discussion of this concept is rather limited.
- Triangulation can, for example, be used for spelling out the idea of using slices of data in a more systematic way.

▮ FURTHER READING

Triangulation and its theoretical basis are spelled out in more detail in the following sources:

Denzin, N.K. (1989) *The Research Act*, 3rd ed. Englewood Cliffs, NJ: Prentice-Hall.

Flick, U. (2018) *Doing Triangulation and Mixed Methods* (Book 9 of *The SAGE Qualitative Research Kit*, 2nd ed.). London: Sage.

Flick, U. (2018) 'Triangulation', in N.K. Denzin and Y.S. Lincoln (eds), *The SAGE Handbook of Qualitative Research*, 5th ed. London: Sage, pp. 444–61.

CHAPTER TEN

ROUNDING UP
DOING PERSPECTIVIST GROUNDED THEORY

CONTENTS

CHAPTER OBJECTIVES

After reading this chapter, you should know:

* how grounded theory overcomes simplifying concepts of emergence;
* how triangulation can be used in grounded theory research to make it multi-perspective; and
* how to design grounded theory research.

PERSPECTIVITY IN GROUNDED THEORY – RESEARCH PROGRAMME OR METAPHOR?

The preceding chapters should have shown several things. Grounded theory is still something of success a story after 50 years 'on the market' of qualitative research. In most contexts, grounded theory is not missing when qualitative research in general is the topic – in handbooks, textbooks, teaching and the like. In some contexts, qualitative research is even equated with grounded theory; in other contexts it is seen as the most prominent or even dominant approach in qualitative research. Grounded theory was the model for developing the most prominent software packages in qualitative research (Atlas.ti and MAXQDA). Citation index searches show the growing use of this term in the literature in various disciplines (see, Hood, 2007, p. 151, for example). At the same time, it is not really clear whether everybody who says to do so is really doing grounded theory. Hood again (2007, p. 163) speaks of the 'Troublesome Trinity' of grounded theory – theoretical sampling, constant comparison of data to theoretical categories and development of theories via theoretical saturation of categories. At the same time she discusses extensively the fact that only a minority of those people who use the term for their research really apply this trinity. And even if grounded theories have been developed in a substantive area, the idea of extending a substantive to a formal theory is very seldom pursued. This is the first level of perspectivity in grounded theory. It is often used as a metaphor for describing some kind qualitative research, using coding, doing qualitative research in a rather open way, using purposive sampling and calling it theoretical sampling, etc. In this case, grounded theory is adopted as a kind of research perspective rather than a research programme in which the methods and elements are applied consistently in the way the programme was originally planned.

RESEARCH PERSPECTIVES IN GROUNDED THEORY

Grounded theory has proliferated over the years into versions according to Glaser, to Strauss, to Charmaz, to Clarke, to Corbin, to Holton, to Morse, to Thornberg, and maybe more. What we find in these versions is a shared core of what grounded theory is about (see Chapter 2, for lists of such key components and integral aspects of the methodology). But at the same time we find a lot of differences about some of the core elements of grounded theory, such as the way of coding (see Chapters 4 and 5), the role of methods in data collection (see Chapter 3), the way and moment of referring to (or even reading) the literature (see Chapter 1), the aim of developing theories (most of the versions) or not (e.g. Clarke; see Chapter 5), the relevance of formal theory as an aim (high for Glaser, low for Corbin) and the like. Bryant and Charmaz (2007c) talk of grounded theory as a family of methods rather than as one method, which could be nailed down to a recipe like in a cookbook. So the second level of perspectivity in grounded theory is that of doing grounded theory according to the various versions that have developed. Here we can take either a mono-perspectivist way and do our research in a Glaserian style or in a strict orientation to Strauss and Corbin, or to Charmaz. Or we can adopt a wider grounded theory concept in a multi-perspectivist way and combine, for example, the idea of coding families (according to Glaser) with the coding paradigm suggested by Strauss and Corbin, or with Charmaz's suggestions for intensive interviewing.

THE RESEARCHER IN THE PROCESS

A third aspect in this context is the role of the researcher in the discovery process. Grounded theory originally started with a strong emphasis on the field and the phenomenon as driving the process of knowledge in the research. That phenomena, categories, relations between them, theories and data emerge from the field was the first understanding of discovery. This implies, on the one hand, that all is already there and you have only to discover it. The role of the researchers is mainly to be open and not misled by preconceptions, by reading other theories and studies, by the impact of methods for data collection and their rules – they should come as a **'tabula rasa'** and then make inductive inferences. This idea of a presuppositionless researcher was behind the original book of Glaser and Strauss and continues to drive the approach Glaser is still vehemently fighting for. In the context of Charmaz's constructivist understanding and Clarke's situationalist/postmodern concept of grounded theory this naïve inductionalism has been abandoned and replaced by an awareness of the role of the researcher in the process of constructing (instead of discovering) grounded theories. It has now been recognized in this context as well, that the influences of the researcher and the way the research is done cannot be avoided (as in any other kind of social research). But it has also been recognized here that the role of the researcher can be actively used to improve the knowledge process in the field. So the third level of perspectivity in grounded theory is to acknowledge the perspective of the researchers in the process as a source of insight and advancing the understanding of the phenomena and the field.

DOING GROUNDED THEORY AS EXPERT OR AS NOVICE

The fourth aspect here is the differentiation of potential researchers' perspectives in a specific way. Glaser and Strauss were experienced researchers when they published *The Discovery of Grounded Theory* (1967). Strauss, for example, was in his fifties at that time. They had been familiar with the areas in which they did their research for a long time. They had already done a number of studies, e.g. Strauss et al. (1964), before they published the book and their concept of research. Much of the book and of the later textbooks by Glaser, Strauss and Corbin, as well as by Charmaz, is based on 'tales of the field' (to borrow van Maanen's, 1988, term). Examples are given, and reported retrospectively, of how the authors proceeded in a specific study, and how the concepts such as theoretical sampling were applied. Larger parts of the books refer to reports of consultations or seminars with analysis sessions. Providing a clearcut, rule-based or step by step orientation for how to plan and how to do grounded theory research plays a relatively small role in the textbooks. Of course, this has much to do with the attitude that is necessary for doing grounded theory in the way this whole approach was set out. This approach is strongly based on the researchers' intuition, which can be seen from various angles.

Grounded theory as systematization of intuition

If we summarize the process of doing grounded theory research as outlined in the preceding chapters, we can see several phases in the research process (Box 10.1). In an *initial phase*, the researchers rely very much on their intuition when they define a field, a problem, get started with first materials and cases. The same is the case in using sensitizing concepts, in initial sampling and the first open coding of materials. The longer they work in the field and with materials, approaches become more systematic and theory oriented – sampling turns into theoretical sampling, coding goes beyond substantive coding towards axial (Strauss), focused (Charmaz) or theoretical (Glaser) coding and thus includes also formal aspects like relations among codes. This is the *conceptual–theoretical phase* of grounded theory research, in which building blocks of a grounded theory are developed, and memos are sorted according to the lines and axes of the developing theory.

Finally, in each approach of grounded theory methodology, selective coding which looks at further evidence for confirming the relevance and centrality of specific categories becomes more relevant. This is the *confirmatory selective phase* of grounded theory development. The last step is the *reflexive phase* in which questions about the theoretical saturation of categories and the theory become relevant. Questions referring to quality criteria concerning the research and the developed theory as its end product are raised in this step.

BOX 10.1 PHASES IN GROUNDED THEORY RESEARCH

- Initial phase.
- Conceptual–theoretical phase.
- Confirmatory selective phase.
- Reflexive phase.

As this description of phases of the research suggests, the process of grounded theory research is based on a large amount of intuition in the early decisions and becomes more and more systematic in its development. This intuitive moment in the research can be applied more effectively the more experience the researcher has. At the same time, it may be the reason why several of the methodological procedures in the process are applied with a lower degree of rigour than in other qualitative approaches and used more flexibly. This also makes it more difficult for novices to learn this approach.

Art and method in grounded theory

This point turns to the tension between art and method in grounded theory research. We find statements such as seeing memo writing as 'a practiced art' (Lempert, 2007, p. 250). Other parts of the research process are difficult to nail down into methodological rules, which can be applied unambiguously. This is the case for theoretical saturation, for developing categories in open coding, for the use of sensitizing concepts and the like. A good grounded theory study is a good combination of art (creativity, flexibility and curiosity towards what is studied) and of methods applied skilfully to reach the goals of the study in a systematic way. This combination can be best learned in working with experienced researchers and scholars of the approach.

This brings us back to the differentiation of researchers' perspectives. The combination of art and method and the reliance on intuition may work easily for experienced researchers (see the stages of expertise discussed in Chapter 8). Both will be quite challenging for novice researchers – for example, facing how to do their first bigger study, e.g. their PhD. As we said in Chapter 8, it could be helpful for this target group to have a bit more orientation on how to plan and do their research. For this purpose, our suggestion of considering and using the concept of research design in grounded theory more extensively could be helpful in early-career-stage research. The same applies to what we said about methods of data collection (see Chapter 3), which is another point that is left a bit vague or narrow in most grounded theory versions and writings. Thus, the fourth level of perspectivity in grounded theory research is the differentiation between the experienced, inner-circle researchers (who may have known Strauss personally or have been working with Glaser for some time) and the other novice users in the research world.

TAKING MULTIPLE PERSPECTIVES SYSTEMATICALLY IN DOING GROUNDED THEORY

The last level of perspectivity in grounded theory research refers to the various perspectives in a field that are relevant for understanding the phenomenon and field and for developing a theory about the issue of the study. In the methodological discourse about grounded theory it has always been said that we need to take various perspectives into account in our studies. However, whose perspectives to include, or how to do this on a methodological level, was left to the researchers in their concrete studies. In their study *Awareness of Dying*, Glaser and Strauss (1965a) talked to all sorts of people (patients, relatives, doctors, nurses, other staff) involved in the process of communication or non-communication about the dying patients or with them. As the authors conceived these conversations as more or less systematic exchanges, there was no need to take several methodological preconceptions for each of these groups. As we said in Chapter 3, it can be helpful to conceive of such conversations as a bit more formalized in the form of interviews. It can also be helpful to apply different forms of interviewing (for example, expert interviews and other forms of interviews with patients or relatives) and combine them in a more systematic way (see Chapter 9). This brings us back to the concept of triangulation of methodological approaches for triangulating the various perspectives. It can also be helpful to not just use conversations and observing the field while being there, but to triangulate interviews to analyze subjective views and to triangulate observations to analyze practices in a systematic way. This allows for combining, comparing and maybe juxtaposing several forms of data in a study, as we discussed in Chapter 9. Finally, we can use the various versions of grounded theory in combination by triangulating the perspectives they take on phenomena to study or to analyze by coding them using open and axial coding, and using coding families and mapping and diagramming in a complementary way.

The five levels discussed here briefly outline what a concept of perspectivist grounded theory can contribute to doing grounded theory in a more systematic and reflexive way, which is less based on the researchers' intuition and experience as prerequisites for using the approach.

● KEY POINTS

- The idea of perspectivity brings a more systematic approach to grounded theory research on various levels.
- This idea refers to seeing the research perspectives in the existing versions of grounded theory.
- It also acknowledges the stronger consideration of the researchers' perspective in constructing grounded theories.
- The idea acknowledges the needs of novice researchers for more explicit advice in the methodology of doing grounded theory compared with experts in the field.
- Triangulation can be used for analyzing the various perspectives in a field in a more systematic way.
- It can also be used to combine the versions of grounded theory and the methodological tools they offer.

■ FURTHER READING

The concept of perspectivity and the underlying methodological issues are spelled out in more detail in the following sources:

Flick, U. (2014) *An Introduction to Qualitative Research*, 5th ed. London: Sage.
Flick, U. (2018) *Designing Qualitative Research* (Book 1 of *The SAGE Qualitative Research Kit*, 2nd ed.). London: Sage.
Flick, U. (2018) *Doing Triangulation and Mixed Methods* (Book 9 of *The SAGE Qualitative Research Kit*, 2nd ed.). London: Sage.

GLOSSARY

Abduction   A kind of reasoning starting from examining inductive data and observing a surprising finding that cannot be explained. Searching for a theoretical explanation involves an imaginative leap to achieve a plausible theoretical explanation. Abduction brings creativity into inquiry and takes the iterative process of grounded theory further into theory construction.

Analytic induction   Strategy for using negative/deviant cases to assess and elaborate findings, models or theories developed.

A priori   Latin expression for 'beforehand'. For example, working with categories defined before entering the field or before beginning to analyze material.

ATLAS.ti   Software for supporting the qualitative analysis of text, images and other data in qualitative research.

Axial coding   A way of coding that treats a category as an axis around which the analyst delineates relationships and specifies the dimensions of this category. Axial coding brings data back together again in a structure after they were fractured in open coding.

Basic design   There are a number of designs that are very typical or used very often in qualitative research and represent a number of different types of research (e.g. case study or longitudinal study).

Benchmark   Cut-off point for distinguishing good/bad or successful/unsuccessful research.

Between-methods triangulation Combination of two independent methods in studying one issue.

Canonization A clear definition of methods by formulating standards for how to apply them leading to a consensus about it and general acceptance of it. For example, by defining rules of how to formulate questions in a specific form of interview.

CAQDAS software Qualitative data analysis software specially developed for supporting the analysis of texts like interviews and their coding, administration, etc. Examples are ATLAS.ti and MAXQDA.

Categorizing To allocate pieces of data with other pieces to one term or headline in order to materialize their similarity, or to different terms in order to materialize their distinctiveness.

Chicago School of Sociology A very influential group of researchers and approaches in the history of qualitative research at the University of Chicago who provided the methodological backgrounds of currently influential approaches like grounded theory. For example, research focused on how the community of (e.g. Polish) immigrants in Chicago was socially organized, how members maintained their cultural identity or adapted to a new one (of being American).

Coding Development of concepts in the context of grounded theory. For example, to label pieces of data and allocate other pieces of data to them (and the label).

Coding families An instrument in grounded theory research for developing relations between codes and for inspiring the researcher in which direction to look for categories.

Coding paradigm A set of basic relations for linking categories and phenomena among each other in grounded theory research.

Comprehensive triangulation Combination of the different forms of triangulation (investigator, theory, methods and data) in one mode.

Concept indicator model A method of theory construction in which the researcher constructs concepts that account for relationships defined in the empirical data and each concept rests on empirical indicators.

Conditional matrix A tool for displaying the wider context, conditions and consequences of actions on micro and macro levels.

Constant comparative method/analysis   Part of grounded theory methodology focusing on comparing all elements in the data with each other.

Constructivism   A variety of epistemologies in which the social reality is seen as the result of constructive processes (activities of the members or processes in their minds).

Credibility   Criterion for evaluating qualitative research based on prolonged engagement in the field.

Criteria   Instruments for assessing the quality of research, ideally coming with a cut-off point (benchmark), to distinguish good from bad research.

Data triangulation   Combination of different forms of data.

Deduction   The logical inference from the general to the particular or, put in other words, from the theory to that which can be observed empirically.

Discourse analysis   Studies of how language is used in certain contexts. For example, how specific identities, practices, knowledge or meanings are produced by describing something in just that way compared to other ways.

Episodic interview   Interview combining question–answer sequences with narratives (of episodes).

Epistemology   Theories of knowledge and perception in science.

Ethnography   Research strategy combining different methods, but based on participation, observation and writing about a field under study.

Ethnomethodology   Theoretical approach interested in analyzing the methods people use in their everyday life to make communication and routines work.

Expert interview   A form of interview that is defined by the specific target group – people in certain professional positions, which enables them to inform us about professional processes or a specific group of patients, for example.

Falsification   Testing theories by trying to show that they are not correct.

Field notes   Notes taken by researchers about their thoughts and observations when they are in the field or 'environment' they are researching.

Focused coding   After initial coding researchers focus on the most frequent and/or significant codes among their initial codes and test these codes against large batches of data.

Formal theory   A more general theory (in grounded theory research) referring to more than one area.

Grounded theory   Theories developed from analyzing empirical material or from studying a field or process.

Hypotheses   In standardized research, assumptions to be tested in research. In qualitative research, hypotheses are used in a more metaphorical sense (e.g. as working hypotheses) without being formulated beforehand.

Indicator   Something representing a specific phenomenon that is not directly accessible.

Induction   Reference from the specific to the general or, in other words, from empirical observation to theory.

Initial coding   The first step of engaging with and defining data. Initial coding forms the link between collecting data and developing a theory for understanding the data.

Institutional review board (IRB)   A committee that reviews research proposals for how far they meet ethical guidelines and standards.

Investigator triangulation   Combination of more than one researcher either in collaboration or independently to promote the quality of the research.

***In vivo* code**   A form of coding based on concepts taken from an interviewee's statements.

Longitudinal studies   A design in which the researchers come back repeatedly after some time to the field and the participants to do interviews several times again in order to analyze development and changes.

MAXQDA   Software for analyzing qualitative data; earlier versions were called WinMax.

Memo   A document written in the research process to note ideas, questions, relations, results, etc. In grounded theory research, memos are building blocks for developing a theory.

Narrative interview Participants are asked to tell the story of their lives (or their illness, for example) as a whole, without being interrupted with questions by the interviewer.

Naturally occurring data Data that are not produced by special methods (like interviews) but are only recorded in the way they can be found in the everyday life under study.

Participant observation The researcher becomes a member of the field under study in order to do observation.

Postmodernism A social theory which criticizes modernism and its concept of facts and science and takes the way science and facts are produced more into account.

Pragmatism A North American philosophical tradition that views reality as characterized by indeterminacy and fluidity, and as open to multiple interpretations. Pragmatism assumes that people are active and creative and meanings emerge through practical actions to solve problems.

Principle of openness A principle in qualitative research, according to which researchers will mostly refrain from formulating hypotheses and formulate (interview) questions as openly as possible in order to come as close as possible to the views of the participants.

Relevance of research How far the research and its results contribute to developing new knowledge or new solutions to specific problems.

Research design A systematic plan for a research project, including who to integrate in the research (sampling), who or what to compare for which dimensions, etc.

Research programme An approach that includes more than a method, such as a concept of reality, an overall strategy, a specific tradition, etc.

Rigour Degree of consistency and consequence in applying a method or in doing an analysis.

Sampling The selection of cases, persons, materials, etc., to study from a bigger population or variety.

Segmentation Decomposition of a text into the smallest meaningful elements.

Selective coding A later step in coding looking for additional material for codes that have been developed before.

Semi-structured interview A set of questions formulated in advance, which can be asked in a variable sequence and perhaps slightly reformulated in the interview in order to allow the interviewees to unfold their views on certain issues.

Sensitizing concepts Concepts that suggest directions along which to look and rest on a general sense of what is relevant.

Site Specific field for studying a process or issue in general, such as an institution, a community, an area, etc.

Substantive theory A more specific theory (in grounded theory research) referring to one area.

Symbolic interactionism A background theory in qualitative research based on the assumption that people act and interact on the basis of the meaning of objects and their interpretation. For example, the use of a computer is influenced by the meaning ascribed to the machine by its users or in the communication about it – as something dangerous, mysterious, practical, or simply a tool for writing more easily and comfortably.

Tabula rasa Latin for 'empty table'. This is used to describe an approach of starting research without reading the literature about the field or the issue and is also used for criticizing this approach. This notion was coined in the beginning of grounded theory research but is no longer held by most researchers in the area.

Thematic coding An approach involving the analysis of data in a comparative way for certain topics after case studies (interviews, for example) have been done.

Theoretical coding The step in grounded theory coding which aims at (further) developing the theory.

Theoretical sampling The sampling procedure in grounded theory research where cases, groups or materials are sampled according to their relevance for the theory that is developed and against the background of what is already the state of knowledge after collecting and analyzing a certain number of cases.

Theoretical saturation The point in grounded theory research at which more data about a theoretical category does not produce any further theoretical insights.

Theoretical triangulation The combination of different theoretical perspectives in the study of one issue.

Transcription   Transformation of recorded materials (conversations, interviews, visual materials, etc.) into text in order to analyze them.

Triangulation   The combination of different methods, theories, data and/or researchers in the study of one issue.

Validity   One of the standard criteria in standardized/quantitative research, analyzed, for example, by looking for confounding influences (internal validity) or for transferability to situations beyond the current research situation (external validity).

Verbal data   Data produced by speaking (in an interview or a group discussion) about a topic.

Within-method triangulation   The combination of two methodological approaches (e.g. question–answer and narratives) in one method.

REFERENCES

Annells, M. (2006) 'Triangulation of qualitative approaches: hermeneutical phenomenology and grounded theory', *Journal of Advanced Nursing*, 56: 55–61.

Atkinson, P., Coffey, A. and Delamont, S. (2003) *Key Themes in Qualitative Research: Continuities and Changes*. New York: Rowan and Littlefield.

Bamberg, M. (2012) 'Narrative analysis', in H. Cooper (editor-in-chief), *APA Handbook of Research Methods in Psychology*. Washington, DC: APA Press, pp. 77–94.

Barbour, R. (2018) *Doing Focus Groups* (Book 4 of *The SAGE Qualitative Research Kit*, 2nd ed.). London: Sage.

Becker, H.S., Geer, B., Hughes, E.C. and Strauss, A.L. (1961) *Boys in White: Student Culture in Medical School*. Chicago: University of Chicago Press.

Benner, P. (1982) 'From novice to expert', *American Journal of Nursing*, 82: 402–7.

Berger, P.L. and Luckmann, T. (1966) *The Social Construction of Reality*. Garden City, NY: Doubleday.

Blumer, H. (1970) 'What's wrong with social theory?', in W.J. Filstead (ed.), *Qualitative Methodology: Firsthand Involvement with the Social World*. Chicago: Markham, pp. 52–62.

Bogner, A., Littig, B. and Menz, W. (2018) 'Generating qualitative data with experts and elites', in U. Flick (ed.), *The SAGE Handbook of Qualitative Data Collection*. London: Sage.

Brinkmann, S. and Kvale, S. (2018) *Doing Interviews* (Book 2 of *The SAGE Qualitative Research Kit*, 2nd ed.). London: Sage.

Bryant, A. (2017) *Grounded Theory and Grounded Theorizing – Pragmatism in Research Practice*. Oxford: Oxford University Press.

Bryant, A. and Charmaz, K. (2007a) 'Grounded theory in historical perspective: an epistemological account', in A. Bryant and K. Charmaz (eds), *The SAGE Handbook of Grounded Theory*. London: Sage, pp. 31–57.

Bryant, A. and Charmaz, K. (eds) (2007b) *The SAGE Handbook of Grounded Theory*. London: Sage.

Bryant, A. and Charmaz, K. (2007c) 'Introduction: grounded theory research: methods and practices', in A. Bryant and K. Charmaz (eds), *The SAGE Handbook of Grounded Theory*. London: Sage, pp. 1–28.

Bryman, A. (2007) 'The research question in social research: what is its role?', *International Journal of Social Research Methodology*, 10: 5–20.

Buscatto, M. (2018) 'Doing ethnography – ways and reasons', in U. Flick (ed.), *The SAGE Handbook of Qualitative Data Collection*. London: Sage.

Charmaz, K. (1997) 'Identity dilemmas of chronically ill men', in A. Strauss and J. Corbin (eds.), *Grounded Theory in Practice*. London: Sage, pp. 35–62.

Charmaz, K. (2003) 'Grounded theory', in J.A. Smith (ed.), *Qualitative Psychology: A Practical Guide to Research Methods*. London: Sage, pp. 81–110.

Charmaz, K. (2006) *Constructing Grounded Theory – A Practical Guide through Qualitative Analysis*. Thousand Oaks, CA: Sage.

Charmaz, K. (2008) 'Grounded theory as an emergent method', in S.N. Hesse-Biber and P. Leavy (eds), *The Handbook of Emergent Methods*. New York: Guilford, pp. 155–70.

Charmaz, K. (2011) 'A constructivist grounded theory analysis of losing and regaining a valued self', in F.J. Wertz, K. Charmaz, L.M. McMullen, R. Josselson, R. Anderson and E. McSpadden, *Five Ways of Doing Qualitative Analysis*. New York: Guilford, pp. 165–204.

Charmaz, K. (2014) *Constructing Grounded Theory: A Practical Guide through Qualitative Analysis*, 2nd ed. London: Sage.

Charmaz, K. and Bryant, A. (2010) 'Grounded theory', in P. Peterson, E. Baker and B. McGaw (eds), *International Encyclopedia of Education*, 3rd ed. New York: Elsevier, pp. 406–12.

Charmaz, K. and Mitchell, R.G. (2001) 'An invitation to grounded theory in ethnography', in P. Atkinson, A. Coffey, S. Delamont, J. Lofland and L.H. Lofland (eds), *Handbook of Ethnography*. London: Sage, pp. 160–74.

Clarke, A. (2005) *Situational Analysis: Grounded Theory after the Postmodern Turn*. Thousand Oaks, CA: Sage.

Coffey, A. (2014) 'Analyzing documents', in U. Flick (ed.), *The SAGE Handbook of Qualitative Data Analysis*. London: Sage, pp. 367–79.

Coffey, A. (2018) *Doing Ethnography* (Book 3 of *The SAGE Qualitative Research Kit*, 2nd ed.). London: Sage.

Corbin, J. and Strauss, A. (1988) *Unending Work and Care: Managing Chronic Illness at Home*. San Francisco: Jossey Bass.

Corbin, J. and Strauss, A. (1990) 'Grounded theory research: Procedures, canons and evaluative criteria', *Qualitative Sociology*, 13: 3–21.

Corbin, J. and Strauss, A. (2008) *Basics of Qualitative Research*, 3rd ed. London: Sage.

Corbin, J. and Strauss, A. (2015) *Basics of Qualitative Research*, 4th ed. London: Sage.

Cornish, F., Gillespie, A. and Zittoun, T. (2014) 'Collaborative data analysis', in U. Flick (ed.), *The SAGE Handbook of Qualitative Data Analysis*. London: Sage, pp. 79–93.

Creswell, J.W. (2013) *Research Design – Qualitative, Quantitative and Mixed Methods Approaches*, 3rd ed. Thousand Oaks, CA: Sage.

Creswell, J.W. (2014) *Qualitative Inquiry and Research Design – Choosing among Five Traditions*, 2nd ed. Thousand Oaks, CA: Sage.

Denzin, N.K. (1970) *The Research Act*. Englewood Cliffs, NJ: Prentice-Hall.

Denzin, N.K. (1989) *The Research Act*, 3rd ed. Englewood Cliffs, NJ: Prentice-Hall.

Denzin, N. (2012) 'Triangulation 2.0', *Journal of Mixed Methods Research*, 6 (2): 80–8.

Dey, I. (2007) 'Grounding categories', in A. Bryant and K. Charmaz (eds), *The SAGE Handbook of Grounded Theory*. London: Sage, pp. 167–90.

Dreyfus, H.L. and Dreyfus, S.E. (1986) *Mind over Machine: The Power of Human Intuition and Expertise in the Era of the Computer*. New York: The Free Press.

Dunne, C. (2011) 'The place of the literature review in grounded research', *International Journal of Social Research Methodology*, 14: 111–24.

Eisenstadt, K.M. (1989) 'Building theories from case study research', *Academy of Management Review*, 14 (4): 532–50.

Fendt, J. and Sachs, W. (2008) 'Grounded theory method in management research – users' perspectives', *Organizational Research Methods*, 11: 430–55.

Flick, U. (1992) 'Triangulation revisited: strategy of or alternative to validation of qualitative data?', *Journal for the Theory of Social Behavior*, 22: 175–97.

Flick, U. (1996) *Psychologie des technisierten Alltags*. Opladen: Westdeutscher Verlag.

Flick, U. (2000) 'Episodic interviewing', in M. Bauer and G. Gaskell (eds), *Qualitative Researching with Text, Image and Sound: A Handbook*. London: Sage, pp. 75–92.

Flick, U. (2011) 'Mixing methods, triangulation and integrated research – challenges for qualitative research in a world of crisis', in N. Denzin and M. Giardina (eds), *Qualitative Inquiry and Global Crisis*. Walnut Creek, CA: Left Coast Press, pp. 132–52.

Flick, U. (2014) *An Introduction to Qualitative Research*, 5th ed. London: Sage.

Flick, U. (2018a) *Doing Triangulation and Mixed Methods* (Book 9 of *The SAGE Qualitative Research Kit*, 2nd ed.). London: Sage.

Flick, U. (2018b) *Managing Quality in Qualitative Research* (Book 10 of *The SAGE Qualitative Research Kit*, 2nd ed.). London: Sage.

Flick, U. (2018c) *Designing Qualitative Research* (Book 1 of *The SAGE Qualitative Research Kit*, 2nd ed.). London: Sage.

Flick, U. (ed.) (2018d) *The SAGE Handbook of Qualitative Data Collection*. London: Sage.

Flick, U. (2018e) 'Triangulation', in N.K. Denzin and Y.S. Lincoln (eds), *The SAGE Handbook of Qualitative Research*, 5th ed. London: Sage, pp. 444–61.

Flick, U. and Röhnsch, G. (2007) 'Idealization and neglect – health concepts of homeless adolescents', *Journal of Health Psychology*, 12: 737–50.

Flick, U. and Röhnsch, G. (2014) 'Migrating diseases: triangulating approaches – applying qualitative inquiry as a global endeavor', *Qualitative Inquiry*, 20: 1096–109.

Flick, U., Hans, B., Hirseland, A., Rasche, S. and Röhnsch, G. (2017) 'Migration, unemployment, and lifeworld: challenges for a new critical qualitative inquiry in migration', *Qualitative Inquiry*, 23 (1): 77–88.

Garfinkel, H. (1967) *Studies in Ethnomethodology*. Englewood Cliffs, NJ: Prentice Hall.

Gibbs, G.R. (2018) *Analyzing Qualitative Data* (Book 6 of *The SAGE Qualitative Research Kit*, 2nd ed.). London: Sage.

Gibson, B. (2007) 'Accommodating critical theory', in A. Bryant and K. Charmaz (eds), *The SAGE Handbook of Grounded Theory*. London: Sage, pp. 436–53.

Glaser, B. (1965) 'The constant comparative method of qualitative analysis', *Social Problems*, 12: 436–45.

Glaser, B.G. (1969) 'The constant comparative method of qualitative analysis', in G.J. McCall and J.L. Simmons (eds), *Issues in Participant Observation*. Reading, MA: Addison-Wesley, pp. 216–228.

Glaser, B.G. (1978) *Theoretical Sensitivity: Advances in the Methodology of Grounded Theory*. Mill Valley, CA: Sociology Press.

Glaser, B.G. (1992) *Basics of Grounded Theory Analysis: Emergence vs. Forcing*. Mill Valley, CA: Sociology Press.

Glaser, B.G. (1998) *Doing Grounded Theory: Issues and Discussions*. Mill Valley, CA: Sociology Press.

Glaser, B.G. (2001) *The Grounded Theory Perspective: Conceptualization Contrasted with Description*. Mill Valley, CA: Sociology Press.

Glaser, B.G. (2002) 'Constructivist grounded theory?', *Forum Qualitative Sozialforschung/ Forum: Qualitative Social Research*, 3. www.qualitative-research.net/index.php/fqs/ article/view/825/1792.

Glaser, B.G. with the assistance of J. Holton (2004) 'Remodeling grounded theory', *Forum Qualitative Sozialforschung/Forum: Qualitative Social Research*, 5 (2): Art. 4. www.qualitative-research.net/index.php/fqs/article/view/607/1315.

Glaser, B.G. (2007a) 'Forty years after discovery: grounded theory worldwide. Barney G. Glaser in conversation with Massimiliano Tarozzi', *Grounded Theory Review*, Nov.: 21–42.

Glaser, B.G. (2007b) 'Doing formal theory', in A. Bryant and K. Charmaz (eds), *The SAGE Handbook of Grounded Theory*. London: Sage, pp. 97–113.

Glaser, B.G. and Strauss, A.L. (1965a) *Awareness of Dying*. Chicago: Aldine.

Glaser, B.G. and Strauss, A.L. (1965b) 'Discovery of substantive theory: a basic strategy underlying qualitative research', *American Behavioral Sciences*, 8: 5–12.

Glaser, B.G. and Strauss, A.L. (1967) *The Discovery of Grounded Theory: Strategies for Qualitative Research*. Chicago: Aldine.

Glaser, B.G. and Strauss, A.L. (1968) *Time for Dying*. Chicago: Aldine.

Glaser, B.G. and Strauss, A.L. (1971) *Status Passage*. Chicago: Aldine.

Goffman, E. (1961) *Asylums: Essays on the Social Situation of Mental Patients and Other Inmates*. New York: Anchor Doubleday.

Goffman, E. (1963) *Stigma*. Englewood Cliffs, NJ: Prentice Hall.

Griesbacher, M. (2016) 'Kodierparadigma und Temporal Sensitivity in der Grounded Theory. Bemerkungen zu den "Methodological Assumptions" von A. Strauss und J. Corbin', in C. Equit and C. Hohage (eds), *Handbuch Grounded Theory – Von der Methodologie zur Forschungspraxis*. Weinheim: Juventa, pp. 141–58.

Gubrium, J. and Holstein, J. (2014) 'Analytic inspiration in ethnographic fieldwork', in U. Flick (ed.), *The SAGE Handbook of Qualitative Data Analysis*. London: Sage, pp. 35–48.

Hammersley, M. (1992) *What's Wrong with Ethnography?* London: Routledge.

Hammersley, M. and Atkinson. P. (1995) *Ethnography: Principles in Practice*, 2nd ed. London: Routledge.

Hermanns, H. (1995) 'Narrative interviews', in U. Flick, E. von Kardorff, H. Keupp, L. von Rosenstiel and S. Wolff (eds), *Handbuch Qualitative Sozialforschung*, 2nd ed. Munich: Psychologie Verlags Union, pp. 182–5.

Hermanns, H. (2004) 'Interviewing as an activity', in U. Flick, E. von Kardorff and I. Steinke (eds), *A Companion to Qualitative Research*. London: Sage, pp. 203–8.

Hesse-Biber, S.N. and Leavy, P. (eds) (2008) *The Handbook of Emergent Methods*. New York: Guilford.

Hoffmann-Riem, C. (1980) 'Die Sozialforschung einer interpretativen Soziologie: Der Datengewinn', *Kölner Zeitschrift für Soziologie und Sozialpsychologie*, 32: 339–72.

Holton, J.A. (2007) 'The coding process and its challenges', in A. Bryant and K. Charmaz (eds), *The SAGE Handbook of Grounded Theory*. London: Sage, pp. 265–90.

Holton, J.A. and Walsh, I. (2017) *Classic Grounded Theory – Applications with Qualitative and Quantitative Data*. London: Sage.

Hood, J. (2007) 'Orthodoxy versus power: the defining traits of grounded theory', in A. Bryant and K. Charmaz (eds), *The SAGE Handbook of Grounded Theory*. London: Sage, pp. 151–64.

Huberman, A.M. and Miles, M.B. (1998) 'Data management and analysis methods', in N. Denzin and Y.S. Lincoln (eds), *Collecting and Interpreting Qualitative Materials*. London: Sage, pp. 179–211.

Kelle, U. (2005) 'Emergence vs. forcing of empirical data? A crucial problem of "grounded theory" reconsidered', *Forum Qualitative Sozialforschung/Forum: Qualitative Social Research*, 6 (2): Art. 27. www.qualitative-research.net/index.php/fqs/article/view/467/1000.

Kelle, U. (2007) 'Development of categories: different approaches in grounded theory', in A. Bryant and K. Charmaz (eds), *The SAGE Handbook of Grounded Theory*. London: Sage, pp. 191–213.

Kelle, U. (2014) 'Theorization from data', in U. Flick (ed.), *The SAGE Handbook of Qualitative Data Analysis*. London: Sage, pp. 554–68.

Kennedy, B. and Thornberg, R. (2018) 'Deduction, induction, and abduction', in U. Flick (ed.), *The SAGE Handbook of Qualitative Data Collection*. London: Sage.

Kuhn, T. (1962) *The Structure of Scientific Revolutions*. Chicago: University of Chicago Press.

Kusenbach, M. (2018) 'Go-alongs', in U. Flick (ed.), *The SAGE Handbook of Qualitative Data Collection*. London: Sage.

Kushner, K.E. and Morrow, R. (2003) 'Grounded theory, feminist theory, critical theory: toward theoretical triangulation', *Advances in Nursing Science*, 26 (1): 30–43.

Latour, B. (2005) *Reassembling the Social – An Introduction to Actor-Network-Theory*. Oxford: Oxford University Press.

LeCompte, M.D. and Schensul, J.J. (1999) 'Analyzing and interpreting ethnographic data', in J.J. Schensul and M.D. LeCompte (eds), *Ethnographer's Toolkit*, Vol. 5. Walnut Creek, CA: Altamira Press.

Lempert, L.B. (2007) 'Asking questions of the data: memo writing in the grounded theory tradition', in A. Bryant and K. Charmaz (eds), *The SAGE Handbook of Grounded Theory*. London: Sage, pp. 245–65.

Lincoln, Y.S. and Guba, E.G. (1985) *Naturalistic Inquiry*. London: Sage.

Lofland, J.H. (1974) 'Styles of reporting qualitative field research', *American Sociologist*, 9: 101–11.

MacDougall, C. and Darbyshire, P. (2018) 'Collecting qualitative data with children', in U. Flick (ed.), *The SAGE Handbook of Qualitative Data Collection*. London: Sage.

Mark, M. (2015) 'Quantitatively driven approaches to multi- and mixed-methods research', in S. Hesse-Biber and R.B. Johnson (eds), *The Oxford Handbook of Multimethod and Mixed Methods Research Inquiry*. Oxford: Oxford University Press, pp. 21–41.

Mauthner, M., Birch, M., Jessop, J. and Miller, T. (eds) (2002) *Ethics in Qualitative Research*. London: Sage.

Maxwell, J.A. (2013) *Qualitative Research Design – An Interactive Approach*, 3rd ed. Thousand Oaks, CA: Sage.

McMullen, L. (2011) 'A discursive analysis of Teresa's protocol: enhancing oneself, diminishing others', in F.J. Wertz, K. Charmaz, L.M. McMullen, R. Josselson, R. Anderson and E. McSpadden, *Five Ways of Doing Qualitative Analysis*. New York: Guilford, pp. 205–23.

Morse, J.M. (1998) 'Designing funded qualitative research', in N. Denzin and Y.S. Lincoln (eds), *Strategies of Qualitative Research*. London: Sage, pp. 56–85.

Morse, J.M. (2007) 'Sampling in grounded theory', in A. Bryant and K. Charmaz (eds), *The SAGE Handbook of Grounded Theory*. London: Sage, pp. 229–44.

Morse, J.M., Stern, P.N., Corbin, J., Bowers, B., Charmaz, K. and Clarke, A.E. (eds) (2009) *Developing Grounded Theory: The Second Generation*. Walnut Creek, CA: Left Coast Press.

Patton, M.Q. (2015) *Qualitative Evaluation and Research Methods*, 4th ed. London: Sage.

Peirce, C.S. (1878/1958) *Collected Papers*. Cambridge, MA: Harvard University Press.

Plummer, K. (2001) *Documents of Life 2: An Invitation to a Critical Humanism*. London: Sage.

Potter, J. and Shaw, C. (2018) 'Naturally occurring data', in U. Flick (ed.), *The SAGE Handbook of Qualitative Data Collection*. London: Sage.

Prior, L. (2003) *Using Documents in Social Research*. London: Sage.

Ragin, C.C. (1994) *Constructing Social Research*. Thousand Oaks, CA: Pine Forge Press.

Rapley, T. (2018) *Doing Conversation, Discourse and Document Analysis* (Book 7 of *The SAGE Qualitative Research Kit*, 2nd ed.). London: Sage.

Rapley, T. and Rees, G. (2018) 'Sampling', in U. Flick (ed.), *The SAGE Handbook of Qualitative Data Collection*. London: Sage.

Reichertz, J. (2007) 'Abduction: the logic of discovery of grounded theory', in A. Bryant and K. Charmaz (eds), *The SAGE Handbook of Grounded Theory*. London: Sage, pp. 214–28.

Rennie, D. (2000) 'Grounded theory methodology as methodological hermeneutics: reconciling realism and relativism', *Theory and Psychology*, 10: 481–502.

Richardson, L. (1994) 'Writing: a method of inquiry', in N. Denzin and Y.S. Lincoln (eds), *Handbook of Qualitative Research*. London: Sage, pp. 516–29.

Riemann, G. and Schütze, F. (1987) 'Trajectory as a basic theoretical concept for analyzing suffering and disorderly social processes', in D. Maines (ed.), *Social Organization and Social Process: Essays in Honor of Anselm Strauss*. New York: Aldine de Gruyter, pp. 333–57.

Rosenthal, G. (2004) 'Biographical research', in C. Seale, G. Gobo, J. Gubrium and D. Silverman (eds), *Qualitative Research Practice*. London: Sage, pp. 48–65.

Roulston, K. (2014) 'Analyzing interviews', in U. Flick (ed.), *The SAGE Handbook of Qualitative Data Analysis*. London: Sage, pp. 297–312.

Roulston, K. and Choi, M. (2018) 'Qualitative interviews', in U. Flick (ed.), *The SAGE Handbook of Qualitative Data Collection*. London: Sage.

Scott, J. (1990) *A Matter of Record: Documentary Sources in Social Research*. Cambridge: Polity Press.

Spradley, J.P. (1980) *Participant Observation*. New York: Rinehart and Winston.

Strauss, A.L. (1987) *Qualitative Analysis for Social Scientists*. New York: Cambridge University Press.

Strauss, A.L. and Corbin, J. (1990) *Basics of Qualitative Research: Grounded Theory Procedures and Techniques*. Newbury Park, CA: Sage.

Strauss, A. and Corbin, J. (1994) 'Grounded theory methodology: an overview', in N.K. Denzin and Y.S. Lincoln (eds), *Handbook of Qualitative Research*. Thousand Oaks, CA: Sage, pp. 273–85.

Strauss, A.L. and Corbin, J. (1998) *Basics of Qualitative Research*, 2nd ed. London: Sage.

Strauss, A.L. and Corbin, J. (2016) 'Methodological assumptions', in C. Equit and C. Hohage (eds), *Handbuch Grounded Theory – Von der Methodologie zur Forschungspraxis*. Weinheim: Juventa, pp. 128–40.

Strauss, A.L., Schatzmann, L., Bucher, R., Ehrlich, D. and Sabshin, M. (1964) *Psychiatric Ideologies and Institutions*. New York: Free Press.

Thornberg, R. (2012) 'Informed grounded theory', *Scandinavian Journal of Educational Research*, 55 (1): 1–17.

Thornberg, R. and Charmaz, K. (2014) 'Grounded theory and theoretical coding', in U. Flick (ed.), *The SAGE Handbook of Qualitative Data Analysis*. London: Sage, pp. 153–69.

Toerien, M. (2014) 'Conversations and conversation analysis', in U. Flick (ed.), *The SAGE Handbook of Qualitative Data Analysis*. London: Sage, pp. 327–40.

Ulrich, C.G. (1999) 'Deutungsmusteranalyse und diskursives Interview', *Zeitschrift für Soziologie*, 28: 429–47.

Van Maanen, J. (1988) *Tales of the Field: On Writing Ethnography*. Chicago: University of Chicago Press.

Wertz, F.J., Charmaz, K., McMullen, L.M., Josselson, R., Anderson, R. and McSpadden, E. (2011) *Five Ways of Doing Qualitative Analysis*. New York: Guilford.

Wiener, C. (2007) 'Making teams work in conducting grounded theory', in A. Bryant and K. Charmaz (eds), *The SAGE Handbook of Grounded Theory*. London: Sage, pp. 293–310.

Wilson, H.S. and Hutchinson, S.A. (1991) 'Triangulation of methods: Heideggerian hermeneutics and grounded theory', *Qualitative Health Research*, 1: 263–76.

Wolff, S. (1987) 'Rapport und Report. Über einige Probleme bei der Erstellung plausibler ethnographischer Texte', in W.v.d. Ohe (ed.), *Kulturanthropologie: Beiträge zum Neubeginn einer Disziplin*. Berlin: Reimer, pp. 333–64.

Wright, H. (2009) 'Using an "emergent design" to study adult education', *Educate – Special Issue*, Dec.: 62–73.

INDEX